DBKDA 2019

The 9 International Conference on Advances in Databases, Knowledge, and Data Applications

June 2 - 6, 2019

Athens, Greece

DBKDA 2019 Editors

Fritz Laux, Reutlingen University, Germany
Lisa Ehrlinger, Johannes Kepler University Linz, Austria / Software Competence Center Hagenberg GmbH, Austria

Printed from e-media with permission by:

Curran Associates, Inc.
57 Morehouse Lane
Red Hook, NY 12571

Some format issues inherent in the e-media version may also appear in this print version.

Printed by Curran Associates, Inc. (2019)

International Academy, Research, and Industry Association (IARIA)
412 Derby Way
Wilmington, DE 19810

Phone: (408) 893-6407
Fax: (408) 527-6351

petre@iaria.org

Additional copies of this publication are available from:

Curran Associates, Inc.
57 Morehouse Lane
Red Hook, NY 12571 USA
Phone: 845-758-0400
Fax: 845-758-2633
Email: curran@proceedings.com
Web: www.proceedings.com

Table of Contents

Utilizing Citation Context in a Two-Level Topic Model for Knowledge Discovery 1
Lixue Zou, Li Wang, and Xiwen Liu

A Schema Readability Metric for Automated Data Quality Measurement 4
Lisa Ehrlinger, Gudrun Huszar, and Wolfram Woess

StrongDBMS: Built from Immutable Components 11
Malcolm Crowe, Santiago Matalonga, and Martti Laiho

A Denormalization Approach to Answering Join Queries 17
Mohammed Hamdi, Kavya Narne, Hamzah Arishi, Feng Yu, and Wen-Chi Hou

Graph Learning for Prediction of Drug-Disease Interactions: Preliminary Results 28
Andrej Kastrin and Dimitar Hristovski

Exploring and Comparing Table Fragments With Fragment Summaries 31
Fatma-Zohra Hannou, Bernd Amann, and Mohamed-Amine Baazizi

A Context Data Metamodel for Distributed Middleware Platforms in Smart Cities 39
Julio Lopes, Lucas Silva, and Gledson Elias

Strongly Possible Keys in Incomplete Databases with Limited Domains 46
Munqath Alattar and Attila Sali

A Skyline Query Processing Approach over Interval Uncertain Data Stream with K-Means Clustering Technique 51
Zarina Dzolkhifli, Hamidah Ibrahim, Fatimah Sidi, Lilly Suriani Affendey, Siti Nurulain Mohd Rum, and Ali Amer Alwan

Towards a Knowledge Graph to Describe and Process Data Defects 57
Joao Marcelo Borovina Josko, Lisa Ehrlinger, and Wolfram Woss

DBKDA 2019

Forward

The Eleventh International Conference on Advances in Databases, Knowledge, and Data Applications (DBKDA 2019), held between June 02, 2019 to June 06, 2019 - Athens, Greece, continued a series of international events covering a large spectrum of topics related to advances in fundamentals on databases, evolution of relation between databases and other domains, data base technologies and content processing, as well as specifics in applications domains databases.

Advances in different technologies and domains related to databases triggered substantial improvements for content processing, information indexing, and data, process and knowledge mining. The push came from Web services, artificial intelligence, and agent technologies, as well as from the generalization of the XML adoption.

High-speed communications and computations, large storage capacities, and load-balancing for distributed databases access allow new approaches for content processing with incomplete patterns, advanced ranking algorithms and advanced indexing methods.

Evolution on e-business, ehealth and telemedicine, bioinformatics, finance and marketing, geographical positioning systems put pressure on database communities to push the 'de facto' methods to support new requirements in terms of scalability, privacy, performance, indexing, and heterogeneity of both content and technology.

We welcomed academic, research and industry contributions. The conference had the following tracks:

- Knowledge and decision base
- Databases technologies
- Data management
- GraphSM: Large-scale Graph Analysis, Management and Applications

We take here the opportunity to warmly thank all the members of the DBKDA 2019 technical program committee, as well as all the reviewers. The creation of such a high quality conference program would not have been possible without their involvement. We also kindly thank all the authors who dedicated much of their time and effort to contribute to DBKDA 2019. We truly believe that, thanks to all these efforts, the final conference program consisted of top quality contributions.

We also thank the members of the DBKDA 2019 organizing committee for their help in handling the logistics and for their work that made this professional meeting a success.

We hope that DBKDA 2019 was a successful international forum for the exchange of ideas and results between academia and industry and to promote further progress in the areas of databases, knowledge and data applications. We also hope that Athens, Greece provided a pleasant environment during the conference and everyone saved some time to enjoy the historic charm of the city.

DBKDA 2019 Chairs

DBKDA Steering Committee
Friedrich Laux, Reutlingen University, Germany
Andreas Schmidt, Karlsruhe Institute of Technology / University of Applied Sciences
Florin Rusu, University of California Merced, USA
Jerzy Grzymala-Busse, University of Kansas, USA
Filip Zavoral, Charles University Prague, Czech Republic
Konstantinos Kalpakis, University of Maryland Baltimore County, USA

DBKDA Industry/Research Advisory Committee
Peter Kieseberg, St. Pölten University of Applied Sciences, Austria
Shin-ichi Ohnishi, Hokkai-Gakuen University, Japan
Thomas Triplet, Ciena inc. / Polytechnique Montreal, Canada
Stephanie Teufel, iimt - international institute of management in technology | University of Fribourg, Switzerland
Rajasekar Karthik, Oak Ridge National Laboratory, USA
Erik Hoel, Esri, USA
Lisa Ehrlinger, Johannes Kepler University Linz, Austria / Software Competence Center Hagenberg GmbH, Austria
Daniel Kimmig, solute GmbH, Germany

DBKDA 2019
Committee

DBKDA Steering Committee

Friedrich Laux, Reutlingen University, Germany
Andreas Schmidt, Karlsruhe Institute of Technology / University of Applied Sciences
Florin Rusu, University of California Merced, USA
Jerzy Grzymala-Busse, University of Kansas, USA
Filip Zavoral, Charles University Prague, Czech Republic
Konstantinos Kalpakis, University of Maryland Baltimore County, USA

DBKDA Industry/Research Advisory Committee

Peter Kieseberg, St. Pölten University of Applied Sciences, Austria
Shin-ichi Ohnishi, Hokkai-Gakuen University, Japan
Thomas Triplet, Ciena inc. / Polytechnique Montreal, Canada
Stephanie Teufel, iimt - international institute of management in technology | University of Fribourg, Switzerland
Rajasekar Karthik, Oak Ridge National Laboratory, USA
Erik Hoel, Esri, USA
Lisa Ehrlinger, Johannes Kepler University Linz, Austria / Software Competence Center Hagenberg GmbH, Austria
Daniel Kimmig, solute GmbH, Germany

DBKDA 2019 Technical Program Committee

Taher Omran Ahmed, Aljabal Algharby University, Azzentan, Libya / College of Applied Sciences, Ibri, Sultanate of Oman
Baris Aksanli, San Diego State University, USA
Markus Aleksy, ABB AG, Germany
Ioannis Anagnostopoulos, University of Thessaly, Greece
Jose L. Arciniegas H., Universidad del Cauca, Columbia
Zeyar Aung, Masdar Institute of Science and Technology, UAE
Gilbert Babin, HEC Montréal, Canada
Edmon Begoli, Oak Ridge National Laboratory / The University of Tennessee, Knoxville, USA
Amel Borgi, University of Tunis El Manar, Tunisia
Zouhaier Brahmia, University of Sfax, Tunisia
Erik Buchmann, Hochschule für Telekommunikation Leipzig, Germany
Martine Cadot, LORIA-Nancy, France
Gabriel Campero Durand, University of Magdeburg, Germany
Ricardo Campos, Polytechnic Institute of Tomar, Portugal
Paola Carrara, CNR IREA, Italy
Chin-Chen Chang, Feng Chia University, Taiwan
Yung Chang Chi, National Cheng Kung University, Taiwan

Byron Choi, Hong Kong Baptist University, Hong Kong
Malcolm Crowe, University of the West of Scotland, UK
Gabriel David, INESC TEC | University of Porto, Portugal
Maria del Pilar Angeles, UNAM, Mexico
Konstantinos Demertzis, Democritus University of Thrace, Greece
Vincenzo Deufemia, University of Salerno, Italy
Juliette Dibie, AgroParisTech, France
Efrén Díez Jiménez, Universidad de Alcalá, Spain
Cedric du Mouza, CNAM, Paris
Lisa Ehrlinger, Johannes Kepler University Linz, Austria / Software Competence Center Hagenberg GmbH, Austria
Gledson Elias, Federal University of Paraíba (UFPB), Brazil
Manuel Filipe Santos, Universidade do Minho | Research Centre Algoritmi, Portugal
Ingrid Fischer, Universität Konstanz, Germany
Sainyam Galhotra, University of Massachusetts Amherst, USA
Barbara Gallina, Mälardalen University, Sweden
Faïez Gargouri, University of Sfax, Tunisia
Pedro Gil Madrona, UCLM, Spain
Shenoda Guirguis, LinkedIn Co, USA
Ana González-Marcos, Universidad de La Rioja, Spain
Bernard Grabot, Ecole Nationale d'Ingénieurs de Tarbes, France
William Grosky, University of Michigan-Dearborn, USA
Jerzy Grzymala-Busse, University of Kansas, USA
Robert Gwadera, Cardiff University, UK
Dirk Habich, Technische Universität Dresden, Germany
Erik Hoel, Esri, USA
Martin Hoppen, Institute for Man-Machine Interaction - RWTH Aachen University, Germany
Ali Hurson, Missouri University of Science and Technology, USA
Hamidah Ibrahim, Universiti Putra Malaysia, Malaysia
Abdessamad Imine, INRIA-LORIA Nancy Grand-Est, France
Vladimir Ivančević, University of Novi Sad, Serbia
Wassim Jaziri, Taibah University, KSA
Imed Kacem, Université de Lorraine, France
György Kálmán, Norwegian University of Science and Technology (NTNU)/mnemonic AS, Research Group on Critical Infrastructure Protection, Norway
Konstantinos Kalpakis, University of Maryland Baltimore County, USA
Verena Kantere, University of Geneva, Switzerland
Benjamin Karsin, University of Hawaii, USA
Rajasekar Karthik, Oak Ridge National Laboratory, USA
Timo Kehrer, Humboldt-Universität zu Berlin, Germany
Peter Kieseberg, St. Pölten University of Applied Sciences, Austria
Daniel Kimmig, solute GmbH, Germany
Petr Křemen, Czech Technical University in Prague, Czech Republic
Anne Laurent, University of Montpellier, France

Friedrich Laux, Reutlingen University, Germany
Martin Ledvinka, Czech Technical University in Prague, Czech Republic
Lenka Lhotska, Czech Institute of Informatics, Robotics and Cybernetics | Czech Technical University in Prague, Czech Republic
Chu-Ti Lin, National Chiayi University, Taiwan
Jerry Chun-Wei Lin, Harbin Institute of Technology, China
Tobias Lindaaker, Neo4j Inc., Sweden
Chunmei Liu, Howard University, USA
Yanjun Liu, Feng Chia University, Taiwan
Shangyu Luo, Rice University, USA
Stephane Maag, Telecom SudParis, France
Tanu Malik, DePaul University, USA
Andrea Marino, University of Pisa, Italy
Gerasimos Marketos, Hellenic Open University, Greece
Elio Masciari, ICAR-CNR, Italy
Michele Melchiori, Università degli Studi di Brescia, Italy
Fabio Mercorio, University of Milan - Bicocca, Italy
Mario Mezzanzanica, University of Milan Bicocca, Italy
Cristian Mihaescu, University of Craiova, Romania
Mohamed Mkaouar, ISAAS, Tunisia
Francesc D. Muñoz-Escoí, Universitat Politècnica de València (UPV), Spain
Lammari Ilham Nadira, Conservatoire National des Arts et Métiers, France
Khaled M. Nagi, Alexandria University, Egypt
Joshua C. Nwokeji, Gannon University - Erie Pennsylvania, USA
Shin-ichi Ohnishi, Hokkai-Gakuen University, Japan
Benoît Otjacques, LIST - Luxembourg Institute of Science and Technology, Luxembourg
Francesco Parisi, University of Calabria, Italy
Shirish Patil, Sitek Inc., USA
Bernhard Peischl, Institute for Software Technology | Graz University of Technology, Austria
Hai Phan, New Jersey Institute of Technology, USA
Gianvito Pio, University of Bari Aldo Moro, Italy
Elaheh Pourabbas, National Research Council | Institute of Systems Analysis and Computer Science "Antonio Ruberti", Italy
Praveen R. Rao, University of Missouri-Kansas City, USA
Manjeet Rege, University of St. Thomas, USA
Jan Richling, South Westphalia University of Applied Sciences, Germany
Marta Rukoz, Université Paris Dauphine, France
Miguel Romero, University of Oxford, UK
Florin Rusu, University of California Merced, USA
M. Saravanan, Ericsson Research, India
Idrissa Sarr, Université Cheikh Anta Diop, Dakar, Sénégal
Andreas Schmidt, Karlsruhe Institute of Technology / University of Applied Sciences Karlsruhe, Germany
Sebastian Schrittwieser, TARGET Research Center, Austria

Copyright Information

Utilizing Citation Context in a Two-Level Topic Model for Knowledge Discovery

Lixue Zou, Li Wang, Xiwen Liu
National Science Library, Chinese Academy of Sciences
University of Chinese Academy of Sciences
Beijing, China
E-mail: zoulx@mail.las.ac.cn, wangli@mail.las.ac.cn, liuxw@mail.las.ac.cn

***Abstract*—Knowledge discovery from academic articles has received increasing attention since full text has been made available by the development of the digital databases. In a corpus of scientific articles, documents are connected by citations and one document has two different parts in the corpus: citation context and autonomous text. We believe that the topic distributions of these two parts are different and related in a certain way. In the existing topic models, little effort is made to incorporate the citation context. In this paper, we propose a citation context topic model which considers the corpus at two levels: cited topic level and citing topic level, utilizing citation context extracted from the full text. Each document has two different representations in the latent topic space. We apply our model to a dataset of PubMed Central, where the full text is available from the XML data. The results clearly show that the citation context can help to discover the latent two-level topics and demonstrate a very promising knowledge discovery capability.**

Keywords-Topic model; Citation context; Knowledge Discovery; XML data.

I. INTRODUCTION

Proliferation of large electronic document collections in the recent past has posed several interesting challenges in knowledge discovery. Latent topic models, such as Probabilistic Latent Semantic Analysis (PLSA) [1] and Latent Dirichlet Allocation (LDA) [2], have become very popular as completely unsupervised techniques for topic discovery in large document collections. These approaches model the co-occurrence patterns present in text and identify a probabilistic membership of the words and the documents in the lower-dimensional topic space [3].

Then, variants of PLSA and LDA allow incorporating more aspects of articles, and here we consider the citation information. As an extension of PLSA, Probabilistic Hypertext-Induced Topic Selection (PHITS) [4] proposed a topical clustering of citations in a manner similar to the topical clustering of words proposed in PLSA, while PLSA-PHITS [5] performed a simultaneous modeling of the citations associated with word occurrences. The Bayesian version of PHITS was proposed as mixed membership model and linked-LDA [6]. In addition, the Citation Network Topic Model (CNTM) [7] presented a non-parametric extension of a combination of the Poisson mixed-topic link model and the author-topic model.

There is also existing work on modeling citation influence. The Copycat and the Citation Influence Model (CIM) [8] introduced the influence parameter to determine how the cited papers are blended into the citing document. The Pairwise-Link-LDA model combines the ideas of LDA and Mixed Membership Block Stochastic Models, while the Link-PLSA-LDA model combines the LDA and PLSA models, assuming that the link structure is a bipartite graph [9]. Additionally, similar models include the Inheritance Topic Model (ITM) [10], the Bi-citation-LDA [11], the Bernoulli Process Topic (BPT) model [12], etc.

Although current citation related topic models are quantitatively successful in clustering the citations and in identifying the citation influence and transitive property, they overlook how those documents influenced the content of this document. That is, the process of incorporation of the citation information ignores the citation context in which that citation appeared in the document.

In our work, we present a two-level topic model utilizing the citation context in a document to discover the latent topic, called the citation context topic model. We define the citation context for a cited document as a bag of words that contains a certain number of words appearing before and after the citation's mention in the citing document. These words can help identify the major topics in the cited document. Moreover, the citation context does not necessarily portray the entire content of the cited document, but provides a description from the authors' perspective in relation to the citing document's topic. This allows us to identify both the cited topics and the autonomous topics.

The rest of this paper is organized as follows: In Section II, we describe the model and the data we dealt with for analysis. Then, Section III gives the experiments and results. Finally, in Section IV, we summarize this paper and prospect our future plans.

II. METHODS

We assume that when the authors write an article, they often reuse ideas and techniques from references, and then based on the inherited thoughts, they generate their own innovative ideas. Thus, each document can be separated into two parts, the citation context and the autonomous text. Moreover, the citation context can be reflected by the cited sentences, while the autonomous text is composed of words that appear outside the citation context. In other words, the topics of each document include two parts: the "citing topics" from the document itself and the "cited topics" from the citations. Further, we let the citation context or the autonomous text choose to "generate" the topic of a word in the autonomous text by incorporating the Bernoulli distribution into the model, to handle the associations among the autonomous text and the citation context.

Our model assumes the following generative process for each document in the corpus: (1) for the citation context, choose a topic from the multinomial distribution of cited topic conditioned on the document, where the distribution parameter is drawn from a Dirichlet distribution; (2) for the autonomous text, toss a coin s ~ Bernoulli (λ), then if s=0, choose a topic from the multinomial distribution of cited topic; if s=1, choose a topic from the multinomial distribution of citing topic, where the distribution parameter is drawn from a Dirichlet distribution; (3) for each topic, choose a word which follows the multinomial distribution conditioned on the topic with the distribution parameter drawn from a Dirichlet distribution.

Similar to LDA, we also need to infer the posterior probability. Considering that the Markov Chain Monte Carlo sampling methods, such as Gibbs sampling, come with a theoretical guarantee of converging to the actual posterior distribution and the recent advances that make its fast computation feasible over a large corpus, we utilize Gibbs sampling as a tool to approximate the posterior distribution.

We performed our experiments on a dataset of PubMed Central [13], where the full text was extracted from the XML files. The dataset corresponds to brain aging and 246 articles that were cited for more than once were chosen for the test. We extracted one sentence surrounding the citation mentioned in the document as the citation context for each cited document.

For the preprocessing, firstly, we used the tokenization and lemmatization to extract and lemmatize words from the citation context and autonomous text, respectively. Then, we filtered out certain words that were stop words, common words and rare words. We define common words as words that appear in more than 80% of the publications, and rare words are words that occur less than 10 times. Finally, the vocabulary size was 2348 unique words.

III. Results

For each paper, we extracted the citation context and its position in the full text. There were a total of 13858 cited documents with 16316 citation sentences in the collection of 246 articles. In these citation sentences, 8673 sentences were labeled with their location in the full text, which mainly contained four types, introduction (including background), methods, results, conclusion (including discussion). As shown in Figure 1, over two thirds of 8673 sentences were located in the introduction part and the conclusion part, at 30 percent and 38 percent, respectively, whereas those in methods and results made up 20 percent and 12 percent, respectively.

Then, we applied our topic model to the dataset with the number of topics fixed at 10. The parameter was also fixed. One main advantage of the model is the capacity of differentiating the two-level topics. For each paper, we can obtain the topic probabilities at the cited topic level and the citing topic level.

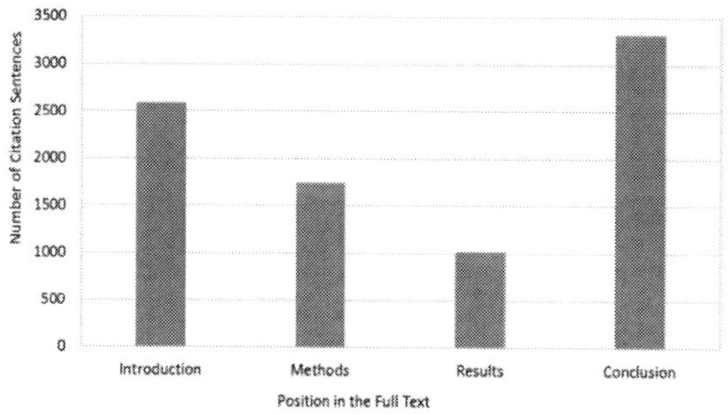

Figure 1. Distribution of citation context in the full text.

Four topics and the top ten words were selected from the output learned by our model, as illustrated in Table I . The topic probability conditioned on the dataset has a high value on "memory" and "mitochondrion and damage" at the cited topic level, while "brain structure" and "dementia" have strong probability at the citing topic level.

TABLE I. DETECTION OF TWO-LEVEL TOPICS

Cited topics	Associated words
Memory	hippocampal (0.069), synaptic (0.054), learn (0.045), plasticity (0.034), receptor (0.034), signal (0.023), impairment (0.020), bdnf (0.015), rodent (0.014), channel (0.014)
Mitochondrion and Damage	mitochondrial (0.032), oxidative (0.030), damage (0.022), neurodegenerative (0.020), pathway (0.018), sirt (0.017), dna (0.016), signal (0.012), antioxidant (0.011), neurodegeneration (0.011)

Citing topics	Associated words
Brain Structure	cortex (0.071), pattern (0.038), cortical (0.0354), rest (0.031), connectivity (0.027), refrontal (0.022), stimulus (0.021), lobe (0.019), neural (0.019), gyrus (0.017)
Dementia	clinical (0.048), dementia (0.044), mild cognitive impairment (0.043), risk (0.033), atrophy (0.031), apoe (0.025), mri (0.025), hippocampal (0.024), diagnosis (0.016)

IV. Discussion and Future Work

In this paper, we propose a citation context topic model to jointly model the generation process of the autonomous text and citation context for each document to discover the two-level topics. The experiment results demonstrate the effectiveness of the model.

In the future, we will test the efficiency of our topic model on a large collection. Additionally, we want to compare with the state of art topic models and evaluate the likelihood performance and the link prediction task. Furthermore, the investigation of the various applications suggests the promising knowledge discovery capability of this model from the full text, such as topic evolution. Wewill couple our method with other bibliometric methods to portray the inherent dependence among topics in the topic evolution.

ACKNOWLEDGMENT

The research reported in this paper has been supported by the Knowledge Innovation Program of the Chinese Academy of Sciences.

REFERENCES

[1] T. Hofmann, "Probabilistic latent semantic analysis," Fifteenth Conference on Uncertainty in Artificial Intelligence, 1999, pp. 289-296.

[2] D. M. Blei, A. Y. Ng, and M. I. Jordan, "Latent dirichlet allocation," J Machine Learning Research Archive, 2003, vol. 3, pp. 993-1022.

[3] S. Kataria, P. Mitra, and S. Bhatia, "Utilizing context in generative bayesian models for linked corpus," Twenty-Fourth AAAI Conference on Artificial Intelligence, 2010, pp. 1340-1345.

[4] D. Cohn and H. Chang, "Learning to probabilistically identify authoritative documents," Seventeenth International Conference on Machine Learning, 2000, pp. 167-174.

[5] D. Cohn and T. Hofmann, "The missing link: a probabilistic model of document content and hypertext connectivity," International Conference on Neural Information Processing Systems, 2001, pp. 409-415.

[6] E. Erosheva, S. Fienberg, and J. Lafferty, "Mixed-membership models of scientific publications," Proceedings of the National Academy of Sciences of the United States of America, 2004, vol. 101, pp. 5220.

[7] K. W. Lim and W. Buntine, "Bibliographic Analysis with the Citation Network Topic Model," Proceedings of the Sixth Asian Conference on Machine Learning (ACML), 2014, pp. 142-158.

[8] L. Dietz, S. Bickel, and T. Scheffer, "Unsupervised prediction of citation influences," International Conference on Machine Learning (ACM), 2007, pp. 233-240.

[9] R. Nallapati, A. Ahmed, E. P. Xing, and W. W. Cohen, "Joint latent topic models for text and citations," ACM SIGKDD International Conference on Knowledge Discovery and Data Mining, 2008, pp. 542-550.

[10] Q. He, B. Chen, J. Pei, B. J. Qiu, P. Mitra, and C. L. Giles. "Detecting topic evolution in scientific literature: how can citations help," ACM, 2009, pp. 957-966.

[11] L. Huang , H. Liu, J. He, and X. Y. Du, "Finding Latest Influential Research Papers Through Modeling Two Views of Citation Links," Asia-pacific Web Conference, 2016, pp. 555-566.

[12] Z. Guo, Z. M. Zhang, S. H. Zhu, Y. Chi, and Y. H. Gong, "A Two-Level Topic Model Towards Knowledge Discovery from Citation Networks," IEEE Transactions on Knowledge & Data Engineering, 2014, vol. 26, pp. 780-794.

[13] PubMed Central, https://www.ncbi.nlm.nih.gov/pmc/ [accessed May, 2019]

A Schema Readability Metric for Automated Data Quality Measurement

Lisa Ehrlinger*†, Gudrun Huszar*, Wolfram Wöß*
*Johannes Kepler University Linz, Altenberger Straße 69, 4040 Linz, Austria
†Software Competence Center Hagenberg, Softwarepark 21, 4232 Hagenberg, Austria
email: lisa.ehrlinger@jku.at, wolfram.woess@jku.at

***Abstract*—Data quality measurement is a critical success factor to estimate the explanatory power of data-driven decisions. Several data quality dimensions, such as completeness, accuracy, and timeliness, have been investigated so far and metrics for their measurement have been proposed. While most research into those dimensions refers to the data values, schema quality dimensions in general, and readability in particular, have not gained sufficient attention so far. A poorly readable schema has a negative impact on the data quality, e.g., two attributes with different purpose, but synonymous labels may cause incorrectly inserted attribute values. Thus, we specifically observe the data quality dimension *readability* on schema-level and introduce a metric for its measurement. The measurement is based on a dictionary-approach using a wordnet, which takes into account the semantics of the words used in the schema (e.g., attribute labels). We implemented and evaluated the schema readability metric within the data quality tool QualIe.**

***Index Terms*—Data Quality; Metrics; Readability; Semantics.**

I. INTRODUCTION

Data Quality (DQ) is a prerequisite to trust data-driven decisions, which can, for example, be strategic decisions in companies, or artificial intelligence algorithms for self-driving cars. Eckerson [1] estimated the costs arising from poor customer data for companies to be more than 600 billion US dollars a year. These costs include failed prints and loss of customers due to incorrect addressing, as well as staff overhead. According to Loshin [2], the primary categories of negative impacts related to DQ are financial (e.g., decreased revenues and increased penalties), confidence and satisfaction-based impacts, productivity impacts (e.g., decreased through-put), and risk and compliance impacts (e.g., investment risks).

Data quality is usually measured in different dimensions, such as, completeness, accuracy, consistency, and minimality [3][4]. Those dimensions can either refer to the extension of the data (i.e., data values), or to their intension (i.e., the schema) [4]. While a lot of research has been conducted for DQ dimensions on the data-level (cf. [5]–[8]), schema quality dimensions in general, and readability in particular, have not gained sufficient attention so far. In existing research, the measurement of readability is usually associated with textual documents and not primarily to Information Systems (ISs). To the best of our knowledge, there exists no metric to measure the readability of IS schemas. Thus, the major contribution of this paper is a discussion of the schema quality dimension readability along with a newly developed metric for its measurement. An essential feature of the metric is the incorporation of semantics of attribute labels using a wordnet.

According to Vossen [9], the quality dimension *readability* describes the condition, in which a schema represents the modeled domain in a natural and clear way, which means, it is self-explanatory to the user. From a more general perspective, the readability of IS schemas is important for two aspects: (1) the understandability of a schema for humans, as described by [9], and (2) the degree to which a schema can be used for automated schema fusion, integration, or matching approaches. An example are two IS schemas within a company, where one schema has a table `product` for storing product types, and the second schema has a corresponding table `prod.Type`, which stores the same entity type. An automated schema integration algorithm requires a sufficient level of readability and standardization in order to merge both tables. Also, an employee, who is not familiar with the schemas, might consider the tables as not equivalent. This scenario could lead on the one hand to duplicate entity types (because both tables are populated separately), and on the other hand to incomplete inventory counts (because only one table is queried for sales statistics). To show the applicability of our readability metric, we implemented it in the DQ tool QualIe [10] and evaluated the ratings of several databases (DBs).

This paper is structured as follows: Section II summarizes related work concerning the measurement of *readability*. In Section III, we present our approach how to measure the readability of IS schemas, with our newly developed metric. The metric is demonstrated and discussed in Section IV. We conclude in Section V with an outlook on future work.

II. STATE OF THE ART AND RELATED WORK

In this section, we provide an overview of related work about readability and explain why existing readability metrics are not sufficiently developed. The DQ dimension readability is most commonly described as the degree to which a schema represents the modeled domain in a natural and clear way, with the aim to be self-explanatory to the user [9]. Since clarity is subjective, no generally valid formal definition for this DQ dimension exists [4]. In alignment with the "fitness for use" principle of DQ [3][11], the readability dimension depends on the intended use and user group. For this definition, the knowledge of the user, the vocabulary and the format of the data is important. In addition to the user perspective, readability is an important aspect for automated schema matching approaches, e.g., in the area of information fusion or information fusion.

When considering the topic from a more general viewpoint, research about the readability of texts in documents has already been published since 1900 [12][13]. In those philology-based approaches, sentence features (e.g., sentence length, syllables in words, word length and popularity) are used to measure the readability of texts. Renzis et al. [14] define readability in this context as the difficulty or simplicity of text comprehension for the intended user. One frequently used index is the Automated Readability Index (ARI) [13], which computes the readability based on syllables per word:

$$ARI = \frac{w}{s} + 9 * \frac{z}{w}, \tag{1}$$

where $\frac{w}{s}$ is the number of words w per sentence s, and $\frac{z}{w}$ is the number of characters z per word. However, Zhao and Khan [12] observed that such philology-based approaches do not consider domain-specific terms sufficiently. For example, *myocardium* is shorter than *myocardal muscle* and thus easier to read with respect to the philology-based approach. The words are synonyms, but a non-expert will rate texts with *myocardium* less readable than texts with *myocardal muscle*. Consequently, readability measures might not represent the "real" readability for non-experts adequately, if domain-specific terms are not considered [12].

However, those philology-based approaches are not useful for measuring schema readability, because instead of sentences, only single words (e.g., attribute labels) are available. While the readability of a conceptual schema in its graphical representation also includes aesthetic criteria, such as the arrangement of entities or crossing lines [15], the readability of a logical schema is limited to the actual naming of entities and relationships.

In the frame of DQ research, Cai et al. [5] observed DQ standards for big data in five dimensions including *presentation quality*, which covers the readability and structure of data representation. Data with high presentation quality allows the user to understand and interpret the data. However, this understanding requires knowledge about commonly used terms, for example, units, codes, and abbreviations. Cai et al. [5] suggested the following indicators to assess the degree of readability in data: (a) data (content, format, semantics, etc.) are clear and understandable, (b) it is easy to judge that the data provided meet requirements, and (c) data description, classification, and coding content satisfy specification and are easy to understand. There is no formal definition of those three indicators, which would allow a direct application to measure the readability in a company IS. The first indicator *clear and understandable* [5] is closely connected with the term *comprehension* from the philological readability definition by Renzis et al. [14]. If a text is clear and understandable, a reader can simply comprehend it. In the context of data, a human can interpret the data and eventually derive information and knowledge.

Yan et al. [16] presented a domain-specific and ontology-based readability measure, which is based on two document properties: cohesion and scope. Cohesion refers to the relatedness of words and is influenced by the association of terms in an ontology. The closer the words in an ontology, the higher is the cohesion. The scope refers to experts knowledge. Assuming $n > 1$, and $i < j$, cohesion is calculated according to [16]:

$$Cohesion(d_i) = \frac{\sum_{i,j=1}^{n} Sim(c_i, c_j)}{NumberOfAssociations}, \tag{2}$$

$$Sim(c_i, c_j) = -log\frac{len(c_i, c_j)}{2D}, \tag{3}$$

$$NumberOfAssociations = \frac{n(n-1)}{2}, \tag{4}$$

where d_i is a document, n is the total number of domain concepts, and c is a concept. $Sim(c_i, c_j)$ computes semantic similarity of concepts. The function $len(c_i, c_j)$ calculates the shortest path between two concepts. *NumberOfAssociations* is the total number of associations among domain concepts.

All mentioned approaches do not provide a definition nor a metric for readability of IS schemas. Thus, we tackle this research issue with a specification of the DQ dimension readability on IS schema-level and a metric to measure it, which is presented in the following section. The approach aims at automated readability measurement, which can be employed for continuous DQ monitoring.

III. An Approach to Measure Schema Readability

In this section, we present our approach to achieve a sufficient level of readability in IS schemas. The approach can be divided into three steps, which are explained in the following subsections: (1) schema preprocessing in order to achieve comparability of different schemas and extract words for the readability calculation, (2) the development of a set of readability criteria, and based on these criteria, (3) the calculation of our readability metric.

A. Schema Preprocessing

For each evaluated schema, a machine-readable description using the Data Source Description (DSD) vocabulary [17] is generated. The DSD vocabulary is an abstraction layer for different schemas. An excerpt of such a DSD file is shown in Figure 1, which contains the description of the `employees` table and the attribute "first_name" from the employees DB [18].

The labels (`rdfs:label`) contained in the DSD files are the basis to extract "words" for further processing. A word can be either the complete label, or part of it. If a schema uses delimiters like underscores (_), hyphens (-), or camel case, one label is split into several words. For example, "first_name" (or alternatively "firstName") is split into "first" and "name". This string splitting enables the usage of each substring of a concatenated label for the readability calculation. One IS schema may consist of several concepts, which are, e.g., tables in relational DBs. In that case, the readability is calculated for

```
ex:employees a dsd:Concept;
  rdfs:label          "employees";
  dsd:hasPrimaryKey   ex:employees.pk;
  dsd:hasAttribute    ex:employees.emp_no,
                      ex:employees.first_name,
                      ex:employees.last_name,
                      ex:employees.birth_date,
                      ex:employees.hire_date,
                      ex:employees.gender.

ex:employees.first_name a dsd:Attribute;
  rdfs:label             "first_name";
  dsd:isOfDataType       xsd:string;
  dsd:maxCharacterLength "14"^^xsd:long ;
  dcterms:title          "first_name" .
```

Fig. 1. Data Source Description of Employees

each concept and the mean of all concept-level readability ratings is used as overall rating for the entire schema.

One challenge faced during this work was the accumulation of duplicate words due to the splitting of concatenated strings. Prefixes and suffixes are a common tool to associate attributes to the respective concepts, e.g., "employeeName" and "employeeNumber". After the splitting, a large number of duplicates (e.g., in this case "employee") is generated and needs to be further processed. We resolved this issue in the implementation by storing all words in a hashmap and, thus, those duplicate words are only considered once.

B. Readability Criteria

For our approach, we developed a set of readability criteria, which are applied to "words". In the following paragraphs, each of these criteria is discussed in more detail and exemplified with the help of a DB for storing employees (cf. Table I). As a result of the readability calculation proposed in this paper, a quality report is produced, which in addition to the readability rating (from the metric) contains a set of annotations that provide further information about the quality of a schema. Figure 2 shows a flowchart diagram of our approach, including the extraction of words from a DSD file, the evaluation of the criteria, and the annotations that are set for each criterion.

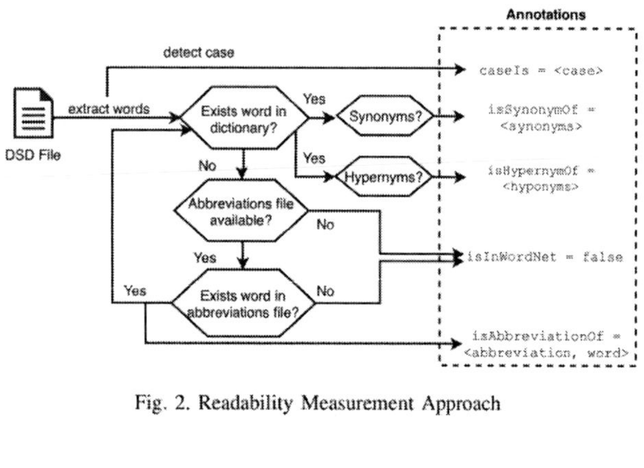

Fig. 2. Readability Measurement Approach

1) Wordnet existence: To detect and process cognates (e.g., synonyms and hypernyms), it must be initially checked whether a word exists in a publicly available online dictionary, and therefore can be considered as generally known. For an automated approach, the usage of a wordnet, which is a combination of a dictionary and a thesaurus, is reasonable. A comprehensive list of wordnets is provided in [19] with prominent examples like DBPedia [20], WoNeF [21], or WordNet [22]. For our approach, we selected the widely used WordNet [22][23], which is developed at Princeton University since 1985. In contrast to a dictionary, the terms in WordNet are categorized into nouns, verbs, adjectives, adverbs, and functors, and are sorted according to their semantics [24]. Terms are grouped to sets of synonyms, so called synsets. The structure of WordNet is based on *psycho-linguistics*, which is the science of the human psyche and explores the task of learning and using a language [25]. A word is annotated with *isInWordNet* (set to true or false) to indicate if it is in WordNet.

If a word was not found in the wordnet, it still may be an abbreviation. Abbreviations can impede readability, because they might lead to ambiguities. An example is the abbreviation *MI*, which refers to *Myocardial Infarction* (heart attack) in the medical context, but could also stand for the state Michigan. Furthermore, there exist ambiguities within a single domain. *MI* can, for example, also refer to *Mental Illness*, a mental disorder of a person. Depending on a persons field of expertise (cardiology or neurology), the same abbreviation would be interpreted differently. In our approach, it is possible to add domain-specific abbreviations, which are frequently used in a specific context, but are not contained in WordNet. This measure is also recommended by Hoberman [15] to increase the readability of conceptual IS schemas.

In QualIe, it is possible to add abbreviations in form of a Comma-Separated Values (CSV) file [26]. If such a file is provided and contains a word, which was not found in a wordnet, the annotation *isAbbreviationOf* is set to link the abbreviation to its corresponding full word. An example is provided in Table I, where a relation for storing employees includes an attribute with the label "emp", which is an abbreviation for "employee". Without additional information, this label would not be found in a wordnet and no further processing (e.g., checking for synonyms) would be possible.

TABLE I. EMPLOYEES TABLE

emp	worker	SALARY	date	product	ware
Doe	Jones	1400	01012010	car	wheel
Smith	Green	1600	01042018	bike	settle

2) Consistent cases: The consistent use of cases is important for a readable schema [15]. Possible variants are uppercase only, initial uppercase, lowercase, camel case, with or without blanks and/or hyphens. If one attribute is written in lowercase and another attribute in uppercase, this might lead to ambiguities. Thus, the inconsistent usage of cases decreases the readability rating. In addition, the annotation *caseIs* gives evidence about the case detected per word. The attribute "SALARY" in Table I is an example for inconsistently used cases compared to the other attributes.

3) Cognates: The semantics, that is, the meaning of the words, is the most important aspect for humans to interpret, understand, and efficiently work with a IS schema. The term *cognates* has its origin in linguistics and describes related words, which have the same origin or share the same meaning, for example, synonyms, hypernyms, or homonyms. Cognates can lead to ambiguities and therefore to a less readable IS schema. Those relations are considered in our readability metric and discussed in the following paragraphs. Josko et al. [27] defined "synonymous values" and "homonymous values" in their formal taxonomy on data defects on IS content-level. We refined the original definitions from [27] to Definitions 1 and 2, to adopt them to synonyms and homonyms within IS schemas.

a) Synonyms: The term *synonym* is derived from the Greek word "syn", which means "together", and describes words, which share the same meaning.

Definition 1 (Synonyms [27]): Let $sp : w(S) \times w(S) \rightarrow \{true, false\}$ be a function that returns if the graphy and pronunciation of two words within S are equal, according to LEX. Let $me : w(S) \times w(S) \rightarrow \{true, false\}$ be a function that returns if the meaning of two words within S are equal or nearly the same, according to LEX. A schema has synonyms *iff* $\exists w_i, w_j \in S$, where $i \neq j$, such that $sp(w_i, w_j) = false$ and $me(w_i, w_j) = true$. Synonyms denote distinct terms in writing that share the same or similar meanings. Such terms can be expressed as vernacular words, acronyms, abbreviations, or symbols. This defect arises when synonymous terms are used interchangeably to indicate the same fact about objects within a schema.

Here, LEX is a universal thesaurus (i.e., a set of lexical definitions, relationships and similarity degrees [27]) and $w(S)$ the set of n words $\{w_1, w_2.., w_n\}$ within an IS schema S. The attributes "product" and "ware" in Table I are synonyms, because the distinction between the two words is not clear. Thus, the existence of synonyms in an IS schema decreases the readability rating. Additionally, the affected attributes are annotated with *isSynonymOf* to link them to their corresponding synonyms.

b) Hypernyms: The term *hypernym* is derived from the Greek word "hyper", which means "above", and denotes a superordinate concept [25]. An IS schema, which includes a specific word (i.e., a *hyponym*), as well as its superordinate concept (hypernym), leads to ambiguities in the interpretation of a schema. Thus, we decrease the readability, if hyponym-hypernym relations are detected. Each hypernym is annotated with *isHypernymOf* to refer to its hyponyms within an IS schema. An example for such a relation is shown in Table I, where "worker" is a hypernym of "employee".

c) Homonyms: The term *homonym* is derived from the Greek word "homo", i.e., "equal", and describes words with the same syntax and pronunciation but different meaning. Thus, homonyms unite the cognates *homographs* (same syntax, different meaning) and *homophones* (same pronunciation, different meaning) [25]. Josko et al. [27] defined homonyms according to:

Definition 2 (Homonyms [27]): Let $sp : w(S) \times w(S) \rightarrow \{true, false\}$ be a function that returns if the graphy and pronunciation of two words within S are equal, according to LEX. Let $me : w(S) \times w(S) \rightarrow \{true, false\}$ be a function that returns if the meaning of two words within S are equal or nearly the same, according to LEX. A schema has homonyms *iff* $\exists w_i, w_j \in S$, where $i \neq j$, such that $sp(w_i, w_j) = true$ and $me(w_i, w_j) = false$. Homonyms are words that sound alike or are spelled alike, but have different meanings. The data defect "homonymous values" arises when homonymous terms are applied interchangeably and indicate the same fact about objects within a schema.

The majority of ISs in productive use implement the relational data model, and therefore lack a semantic annotation of the words within a schema. For example, the meaning of the word "bank", which can refer to the financial institution, or to a river bank, is not explicitly defined. The meaning is only implicitly available through the IS content, or known by domain experts. In such schemas, the distinction between homonyms and synonyms is not possible due to the lack of explicitly available semantics. Therefore, homonym detection is not part of our current implementation. However, more complex data models, like ontologies, would enable homonym detection. Part of our future work is to extend the readability metric with homonym detection.

C. A Metric to Measure Schema Readability

Based on the criteria from Section III-B, we suggest calculating the readability of an IS schema according to

$$Red(s) = \frac{\sum_{i=1}^{|w|} \#\text{fcrit}_i / \#\text{crit}}{|w|}, \qquad (5)$$

where $|w|$ is the total number of words in schema s, $\#crit$ is the number of considered criteria, and $\#fcrit_i$ is the number of fulfilled criteria per word w_i. The metric delivers readability ratings that are normalized by [0,1], where 0.0 represents absolute poor readability, and 1.0 perfectly good readability. This characteristic aligns with the five requirements a sound DQ metric should fulfill by Heinrich et al. [28]. To discuss these requirements with respect to our readability metric, we calculated all possible ratings for a schema with 100 attributes. Figure 3 shows on the left side a boxplot, which indicates the distribution of the resulting metric ratings. On the right side of the figure, a line plot illustrates the metric rating per total number of fulfilled criteria, that is, number of attributes (100) multiplied by number of criteria (here 4: wordnet existence, case consistency, synonyms, and hypernyms).

The first requirement by [28] (*Existence of Minimum and Maximum Metric Values*) states that the metric results have to

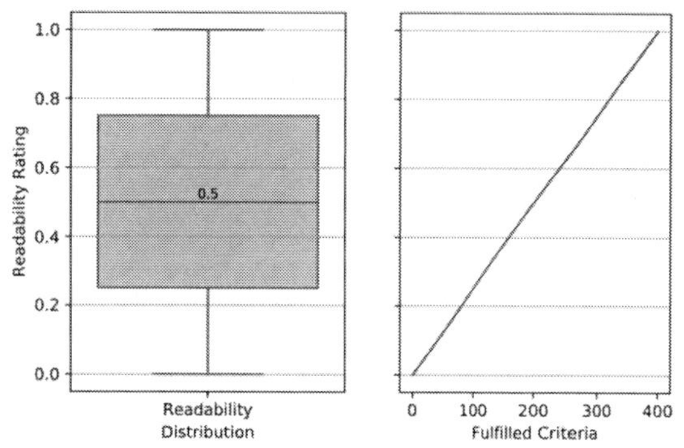

Fig. 3. Readability Metric Results

be normalized by [0,1], where 0.0 represents least readability, and 1.0 best readability. The whiskers of the boxplot in Figure 3 are bound by 0.0 and 1.0, which illustrates the fulfillment of this requirement. The second requirement (*Interval-Scaled Metric Values*) states that the steps of the metric result have to be equally spaced [28]. Both plots in Figure 3 show the fulfillment of this requirement, because (1) the median of all possible readability rating is with 0.5 the exact mean between the minimum and maximum values, and (2) for every fulfilled criteria per word, the gradient is increased with a fixed step size. If the readability rating of a schema is improved from 0.6 to 0.7, this corresponds to an improvement of the readability from 0.2 to 0.3. Consequently, the differences between the units of the metric results are always equally spaced. Although the fourth requirement (*Sound Aggregation of the Metric Values*) originally referred to the aggregation on IS data-level in terms of aggregating record-level QQ to table-level DQ, our metric also allows to aggregate the readability ratings between the single tables to an aggregated value for the entire IS schema. The remaining requirements R3 (*Quality of the Configuration Parameters and the Determination of the Metric Values*) and R5 (*Economic Efficiency of the Metric*) refer to the degree of automation, the parameters for the metric can be determined and measured with. We claim that both requirements are fulfilled, since we showed how to measure the criteria $crit$ in an automated way using WordNet.

IV. Proof-of-Concept Implementation

The readability metric proposed in this paper has been implemented and demonstrated in the Java-based DQ tool QuaIIe (Quality Assessment for Integrated Information Environments, pronounced ['kvɑlə]), introduced in [10]. QuaIIe automatically performs domain-independent quality measurement on both data-level and schema-level. Although the current version of the readability metric in QuaIIe was originally developed for the schema-level, it could be easily modified to assess the readability of string values on the content-level likewise. In this section, we demonstrate the functionality and applicability of our readability metric. For the interaction with WordNet, we used a Java WordNet API developed at the Massachusetts Institute of Technology (MIT) [29].

The selection of data sources for our proof-of-concept demonstration follows the evaluation suggestions for DQ metrics by Sadiq et al. [30], who promoted to use both, common synthetic data sets (for a manual verification of the readability calculation), as well as large real world data sets to show the applicability in practice. Thus, we selected the following DBs: (1) *Alphavantage* is highly volatile real-world stock exchange data, (2) *Chinook* [31] is a relational DB for digital media, (3) *Employees* [18] is a sample MySQL DB with six tables and about three million records that stores employees and departments within a company, (4) *Northwind* [32] is the well-known SQL DB from Microsoft, (5) *Metadynea* is a productive Cassandra DB from one of our industry partners that stores about 60 GB of chemometrics data distributed on three nodes, and (6) *Sakila* [33] is a MySQL sample DB for the administration of a film distribution with a more advanced schema (16 tables) than the employees DB. Table II, which is explained in the following sections, shows the readability ratings for each DB schema.

A. Alphavantage

We collected real-world stock exchange data with the alphavantage API [34], which yields a schema with information about the "time stamp", "open" and "close" date, and the "volume" per stock. The observed table about IBM stock data achieves a quite high readability rating of 0.8750. Lowercases are used consistently in the entire schema. The main reason for the degraded readability is the attribute label "timestamp", which has no exact match in WordNet, because the corresponding entry is "time stamp". No synonyms or hypernyms are detected. However, additional cognates could be detected, if the attribute label "timestamp" would have been split into "time" and "stamp", and both words are found in WordNet.

B. Chinook

The readability of the Chinook schema with 10 tables achieves the second-lowest rating with 0.5172. Lowercase is consistently used in the entire schema. A major point for the low readability are string concatenations. Several attribute labels have the table name as prefix, e.g., "customerid" or "artistid". Here, an automated split during the preprocessing process is not possible, because no delimiter is used. Consequently, those attribute labels are treated as single words, which are not found in WordNet. The highest readability has the table `customer` (0.6731). It includes customer contact data, such as "email", "phone", and "address", where the labels are single words that exist in the wordnet. The two synonyms "state" and "country" decrease the readability further.

C. Employees

The employees schema has a readability of 0.6902. The attribute labels are consistently written in lowercase and several labels are concatenated with an underscore, and therefore

TABLE II. READABILITY MEASUREMENTS

Schema	Readability	Concatenations	Cases	Abbreviations	Synonyms	Hypernyms
Alphavantage	0.8750	no split point	lower	-	-	-
Chinook	0.5172	no split point	lower	-	state ↔ country	-
Employees	0.6902	underscore	lower	-	-	first ← birth
Employees	0.8585	underscore	lower	file provided	-	first ← birth
Northwind	0.4247	no split point	lower	-	-	description ← picture; region ← country
Metadynea	0.9803	underscore	lower	-	-	level ← quality, intensity; time ← hour; type ← version
Sakila	0.9904	underscore	lower	-	duration ↔ length	code ← address; film ← feature

split during the preprocessing. In contrast to Chinook, this word concatenation does not lead to a deterioration of the readability, because both words are individually looked up in WordNet. For humans, the schema is easy readable due to the fact that most of the abbreviations are commonly used. For example, the abbreviations "dept" for departments and "emp" for employees are used as prefixes for attribute labels, such as "dept_name" and "emp_no". However, the abbreviations "dept" and "emp" are not part of WordNet and therefore decrease the calculated readability. This issue can be resolved by including an abbreviations CSV file, which increases the readability ranking to 0.8585 (see Table II). An additional impact on the readability has the fact that "first" is recognized as hypernym of "birth".

D. Northwind

The Northwind DB achieves with 0.4247 the lowest readability rating of all observed schemas, despite the fact that all words are consistently written in lowercase. Analogue to Chinook, the major reason for the low rating are string concatenations without delimiters. Many attribute labels include substrings, for example, "categoryname", "companyname", or "contacttitle". Since no split point can be detected, those concatenations cannot be resolved.

E. Metadynea

The readability of the Metadynea schema is the second-best with 0.9803. All words are consistently written in lowercase and concatenated with underscores, which allows splitting. No unknown abbreviations are used and all words are included in WordNet. The only drawbacks found are several hypernyms, e.g., "time" is a hypernym of "hour".

F. Sakila

The overall best readability rating with 0.9904 is achieved by Sakila, where all words except "username" are included in WordNet. Labels used for attributes are consistently written in lowercase. One minor problem is the attribute label "address2", which can neither be splitted nor has a match in WordNet. Further, several cognates are detected, e.g., the word "code" contained in the attribute label "postal code" is identified as hypernym of the word "address".

V. CONCLUSION

The readability of IS schemas is of particular importance to ensure automated schema integration and to allow humans a correct interpretation of table and attribute names. In this paper, we have introduced a novel metric for the readability of IS schemas, which is based on a set of readability critera that are applied to words extracted from a schema. In the current state, the metric considers the criteria (a) entry in a wordnet, (b) consistency of cases, and the cognates (c) synonyms and (d) hypernyms. To demonstrate the applicability of our metric, we implemented it in the DQ tool QuaIIe and measured the readability of multiple synthetic and real data sources.

In our ongoing and future work, we plan to extend the readability metric with (1) text-based approaches, (2) string similarity, (3) normalization with respect to the schema size, as well as (4) further investigation on string splitting. Since there is a lot of related work about readability concerning text-based approaches, it could also be beneficial to take into account word complexity [13]. Words with many syllables are more complex and a schema with a lot of complex words is less readable. The second possible improvement with string similarity could be used to detect similar attribute names that are only distinguished by a typo, for example, "productNumber" and "porductNumber". Those words would not be considered similar with the presented algorithm, but could be taken into account with string similarity algorithms, like the Levensthein distance. The current implementation does not consider the size of the evaluated IS. Since larger ISs tend to have more (readability) errors, an interesting index could be the consideration of errors per hundred tables. In addition, we think that the challenging topic of splitting strings without a clear split point, e.g., "categoryname", would be worth to be investigated in the future. Last, but not least, we are going to extend and refine the evaluation of our metric by (1) additionally using benchmark data sets for federated ISs, and (2) conducting a user study to compare the readability ratings of the metric to the assessment of real users.

ACKNOWLEDGMENT

The research reported in this paper has been partly supported by the Austrian Ministry for Transport, Innovation and Technology, the Federal Ministry of Digital and Economic Affairs, and the Province of Upper Austria in the frame of the COMET center SCCH.

REFERENCES

[1] W. W. Eckerson, "Data Quality and the Bottom Line – Achieving Business Success through a Commitment to High Quality Data," The Data Warehousing Institute, Technical Report, 2002.

[2] D. Loshin, *The Practitioners Guide to Data Quality Improvement*. Elsevier Inc., 2011.

[3] Y. Wand and R. Y. Wang, "Anchoring Data Quality Dimensions in Ontological Foundations," *Communications of the ACM*, vol. 39, no. 11, Nov. 1996, pp. 86–95.

[4] C. Batini and M. Scannapieco, *Data and Information Quality: Concepts, Methodologies and Techniques*. Springer International Publishing, 2016.

[5] L. Cai and Y. Zhu, "The Challenges of Data Quality and Data Quality Assessment in the Big Data Era," in *Data Science Journal*, vol. 14. Ubiquity Press, 2015, pp. 1–10.

[6] N. A. Emran, S. Embury, P. Missier, M. N. M. Isa, and A. K. Muda, "Measuring Data Completeness for Microbial Genomics Database," in *5th Asian Conference on Intelligent Information and Database Systems*. Springer-Verlag Berlin Heidelberg, 2013, pp. 186–195.

[7] O. Foley and M. Helfert, "The Development of an Objective Metric for the Accessibility Dimension of Data Quality," in *4th International Conference on Innovations in Information Technology*. IEEE, 2007, pp. 11–15.

[8] L. Pipino, Y. Lee, and R. Y. Wang, "Data Quality Assessment," in *Communications Of The ACM*. ACM New York, April 2002, pp. 211–218.

[9] G. Vossen, *Datenmodelle, Datenbanksprachen und Datenbankmanagementsysteme [Data Models, Database Languages, and Database Management Systems]*. Oldenbourg Verlag, 2008.

[10] L. Ehrlinger, B. Werth, and W. Wöß, "QualIe: A Data Quality Assessment Tool for Integrated Information Systems," *Proceedings of the Tenth International Conference on Advances in Databases, Knowledge, and Data Applications (DBKDA 2018)*, 2018, pp. 21–31.

[11] R. Y. Wang and D. M. Strong, "Beyond Accuracy: What Data Quality Means to Data Consumers," *Journal of Management Information Systems*, vol. 12, no. 4, March 1996, pp. 5–33.

[12] J. Zhao and M. Kan, "Domain-Specific Iterative Readability Computation," in *Proceedings of the 10th annual joint conference on Digital libraries*. ACM New York, June 2010, pp. 205–214.

[13] R. J. Senter and E. A. Smith, "Automated Readability Index," United States Air Force Aerospace Medical Research Laboratories, Technical Report, *AMRLTR-66-220*, November 1967.

[14] A. D. Renzisa *et al.*, "A Domain Independent Readability Metric for Web Service Descriptions," in *Computer Standards and Interfaces*. Elsevier, 2017, pp. 124–141.

[15] S. Hoberman, *Data Model Scorecard*. Technics Publications, 2015.

[16] X. Yan, D. Song, and X. Li, "Concept-based Document Readability in Domain Specific Information Retrieval," in *Proceedings of the 15th ACM International Conference on Information and Knowledge Management (CIKM '06)*. NY, USA: ACM, 2006, pp. 540–549.

[17] L. Ehrlinger and W. Wöß, "Semi-Automatically Generated Hybrid Ontologies for Information Integration," in *Joint Proceedings of the Posters and Demos Track of 11th International Conference on Semantic Systems*. CEUR Workshop Proceedings, 2015, pp. 100–104.

[18] Oracle Corporation, "Employees Sample Database," https://dev.mysql.com/doc/employee/en [retrieved: April, 2019].

[19] The Global WordNet Association, "Global Wordnet Association," http://globalwordnet.org/ [retrieved: April, 2019].

[20] DBpedia Association, "DBpedia," http://wiki.dbpedia.org [retrieved: April, 2019], 2018.

[21] "WordNet du Franais," https://wonef.fr [retrieved: April, 2019].

[22] Princeton University, "WordNet - A Lexical Database for English," https://wordnet.princeton.edu [retrieved: April, 2019].

[23] G. A. Miller, R. Beckwith, C. Fellbaum, D. Gross, and K. Miller, "Introduction to WordNet: An On-line Lexical Database," in *International Journal of Lexicography*, vol. 3. Oxford University Press, 12 1990, pp. 235 - 244.

[24] M. A. Finlayson, "Java Libraries for Accessing the Princeton Wordnet: Comparison and Evaluation," in *Proceedings of the 7th International Global WordNet Conference*, H. Orav, C. Fellbaum, and P. Vossen, Eds. Association for Computational Linguistics, January 2014, pp. 78–85.

[25] Oxford University Press, "Oxford Dictionaries," https://en.oxforddictionaries.com/definition [retrieved: April, 2019].

[26] L. Ehrlinger, B. Werth, and W. Wöß, "Automated Continuous Data Quality Measurement with QualIe," *International Journal on Advances in Software*, vol. 11, no. 3 & 4, 2018, pp. 400–417.

[27] J. M. B. Josko, M. K. Oikawa, and J. E. Ferreira, "A Formal Taxonomy to Improve Data Defect Description," in *Database Systems for Advanced Applications*, H. Gao, J. Kim, and Y. Sakurai, Eds. Springer International Publishing, 2016, pp. 307–320.

[28] B. Heinrich, D. Hristova, M. Klier, A. Schiller, and M. Szubartowicz, "Requirements for Data Quality Metrics," *Journal of Data and Information Quality*, vol. 9, no. 2, January 2018, pp. 12:1–12:32.

[29] Massachusetts Institute of Technology, "The MIT Java Wordnet Interface," https://projects.csail.mit.edu/jwi [retrieved: April, 2019].

[30] S. Sadiq *et al.*, "Data Quality: The Role of Empiricism," *ACM SIGMOD Record*, vol. 46, no. 4, 2018, pp. 35–43.

[31] Microsoft Inc., "ChinookDatabase," https://archive.codeplex.com/?p=chinookdatabase [retrieved: April, 2019].

[32] Microsoft Inc., "Northwind and pubs Sample Databases for SQL Server 2000," 2018, https://www.microsoft.com/en-us/download/details.aspx?id=23654 [retrieved: April, 2019].

[33] Oracle Corporation, "Sakila Sample Database," https://dev.mysql.com/doc/sakila/en [retrieved: April, 2019].

[34] Alpha Vantage Inc., "ALPHA VANTAGE," 2018, https://www.alphavantage.co [retrieved: April, 2019].

StrongDBMS: Built from Immutable Components

Malcolm Crowe, Santiago Matalonga
University of the West of Scotland
Paisley, UK
email: {malcolm.crowe; santiago.matalonga}@uws.ac.uk

Martti Laiho
DBTechNet
Helsinki, Finland
emal:martti.laiho@gmail.com

***Abstract*—StrongDBMS is a new relational Database Management System (DBMS). Atomicity, Consistency, Isolation and Durability (ACID) properties are guaranteed through the use of an explicit transaction log and immutable software components. The shareable data structures used allow instant snapshots and provide thread-safety even for iterators, and minimize the need for locking mechanisms without compromising consistency. StrongDBMS has been implemented in C# and Java, and both versions are inter-operable on Windows and Linux. Benchmarking measures are included in this paper. StrongDBMS is open-source and free to use. This paper presents the design rationale for StrongDBMS and benchmarks its current version. Benchmarking results using the Transaction Processing Council's TPC/C benchmark show performance comparable with standard commercial products.**

Keywords– optimistic; relational; thread-safety; transactions.

I. Introduction

StrongDBMS has as its design goal to build a simple fully-ACID relational DBMS, based on an append-only transaction log file, and *shareable* data structures. The transaction log file gives guarantees of transaction isolation and durability, and shareable data structures, as described below, provide guarantees of atomicity and consistency.

The rest of Section 1 gives some background to the work, Section 2 introduces *shareable* data structures, Section 3 describes the resulting database architecture, and Section 4 discusses some benchmarking data on the resulting DBMS.

A. Background

Most modern DBMSs, including StrongDBMS and Pyrrho [1], employ Multi-Version Concurrency Control (MVCC), in which each transaction effectively works with a private copy of the DB. For higher levels of isolation, such as Snapshot Isolation (SI) and Serializable SI (SSI), a transaction which reads a data item x sees a private copy of x with value that it had when the transaction began, and a transaction which writes x does so on a private copy of x which is only made available globally (i.e., to other transactions) upon a successful commit operator of the writer.

However, in most systems, this ideal strategy is made more complex by the sharing of index structures between concurrent transactions, so that many DBMS use the First Updater Wins strategy (FUW) so that the first transaction to announce an update locks the index until it commits [2]. With StrongDBMS and Pyrrho, each transaction uses its own indexes and access data structures, and so these DBMS are able to implement First Committer Wins (FCW), in which transactions proceed without interfering with each other until commit time. Upon commit, if there have not been other commits on objects which T has written or read, it is allowed to commit. Otherwise, T must be aborted. With this approach, integrity constraints against commits made since the start of T cannot be made until T begins to commit.

Both StrongDBMS and Pyrrho use immutable objects with maximal sharing for indexes and access structures. The objects are immutable in the sense that any modification of the value of a data object results in a new object; pointers cannot be updated, and values are never overwritten. The objects admit maximal sharing in that when an object is modified (or a new object is created), that part which is the same as the previous object is re-used; only the part which is different uses new storage.

StrongDBMS extends the use of immutable objects to all serializable objects and all objects used in query processing including row sets, and so these desirable properties can be guaranteed throughout the transaction implementation. The main goal of this paper is to show how such immutable objects with sharing may be used in the implementation of a DBMS.

B. Relationship to previous work

In Pyrrho and StrongDBMS, each database is stored on disk as a single append-only transaction log file. The data format is independent of machine architecture, word size, byte order, or locale. Entries in the log from each transaction are appended as a group for atomicity and serialization, as explained below. Database objects have a unique identity given by their definition point in the log. They retain this identity when updated or modified even though the modification details are recorded later in the log.

In this way, both are optimistic-execution DBMS with persistent row-versioning, as discussed in [3]. Unlike Pyrrho, StrongDBMS is implemented in Java as well as C#, taking advantage of its novel aspects of the features of each programming language, and both implementations can run on Windows and Linux.

StrongDBMS' internal data structures (in the Shareable namespace) are serializable and used both in the server and the client, with a binary API. SQL parser in the client library. There are some system tables that provide relational access to the internal mechanisms of the DBMS.

The DBMS is still under development and many standard Structured Query Language (SQL) features will be added later. It currently supports integrity constraints, aggregation, grouping, and joins. Roles, views and support for "big live data" [4] will be added during 2019, followed by executable modules and triggers.

The data types supported are arbitrary-precision integers and numeric, unicode string, date and timespan, and row. Identifiers are case-sensitive. The set of system tables is currently limited to the log and the list of base tables.

StrongDBMS uses a client-server architecture with a client Application Programming Interface (API) based on serializable objects rather than SQL. Parsing of SQL is performed in the client library (StrongLink). The server, StrongDB, opens a Transmission Control Protocol (TCP) port on 50433. There is a command-line utility StrongCmd. The implementation uses .NET framework 4.7.2, C# version 8.0 (2019), and Java 11. It is open-source and free to use. The source code is on github.com [5], together with an introduction to the serializable classes of StrongDBMS.

StrongDBMS is available for use by anyone and in any product without fee, provided only that its origin and original authorship is suitably acknowledged.

II. Shareable Data Structures

The unique interest of StrongDBMS is the use of shareable (or immutable) data structures. Such structures are particularly appropriate for DBMS, since they are inherently thread-safe, provide instant snapshots, and do not require locking. This section briefly introduces this concept.

A. On value semantics and thread-safety

The study of data structures is an essential early stage in any Computing program [6] and needs to be revisited later on when the student has mastered threading [7]. Students quickly learn that the standard string data type in modern languages, such as Java and C#, is immutable, but are often not told why.

As an unsafe example, consider arrays of characters in Java. Suppose A, declared as char[] A, contains the characters NOW. If we assign this array to a similar array B, then both A and B share the same data. After an update to A, say A[2] = 'T', they *both* contain NOT. This may be what the programmer intended, but from the viewpoint of this study, this behaviour is seen as unsafe. There is nothing wrong with the original assignment of A to B or with sharing the array elements. But A[2] = 'T' represents a problem (and Java wisely disallows such an operation for Strings). So, for a shareable list structure we support A=A.InsertAt('T',2) and A=A.RemoveAt(1), and both these operations create new lists without changing the contents of B. The implementation, of course, will be as a linked list.

This is not to criticize Java, which has built on its String structure and championed interfaces such as Cloneable. Linked lists are not the best structures for databases either, but shareable data structures with logarithmic behaviour can transform the performance of databases.

When a shareable structure such as a linked list or tree is updated, new nodes are required from the start of the structure to the updated position. The rest of the structure is unchanged and does not need to be copied.

Before leaving the notion of thread-safety, consider the behaviour of data structures passed as parameters. Java (as a requirement) and C# (by default) pass parameters "by value", a comfortable phrase that obscures a major source of difficulty. There is nothing to stop the called procedure from modifying a structure passed in. Such modifications are often useful but can be a difficult source of error.

The solution to both problem areas is to use, as far as possible, data structures that contain no mutable fields. In C# and Java, immutable fields can be declared **public readonly** or **public final**; they receive their values in constructors and these cannot be changed. It is a huge advantage that whole indexes and even whole databases in memory can then be copied by a single machine instruction, and database rollback or Prolog Unbind consists simply of forgetting the new pointer. With such data structures, there is no need for locking, because the values inside can never change. Managing locking in complex software has been a problem for many decades (9) and it is a great relief to reduce this burden.

The most commonly used shareable data structure in StrongDBMS is a key-value dictionary called SDict<K,V> , which is used to build shareable searchable arrays (e.g., SDict<int,bool>) and multi-level indexes that use such dictionaries at each level. In C#, it is possible to define operators so that we can use d += (k,v) for adding an entry to dictionary d, which is safer than having to remember to write d= d.Add(k,v) . (Java's dictionaries are not safe, and many programmers used to them will accidentally write d.Add(k,v) and lose the updated dictionary.)

Instead of using linear linked lists or arrays, for scalability it is strongly recommended to use structures with logarithmic behaviour such as B-Trees. Figure 1 shows the picture of an update for a B-tree, reproduced from [8], and shows that only a few nodes need to be created on an update.

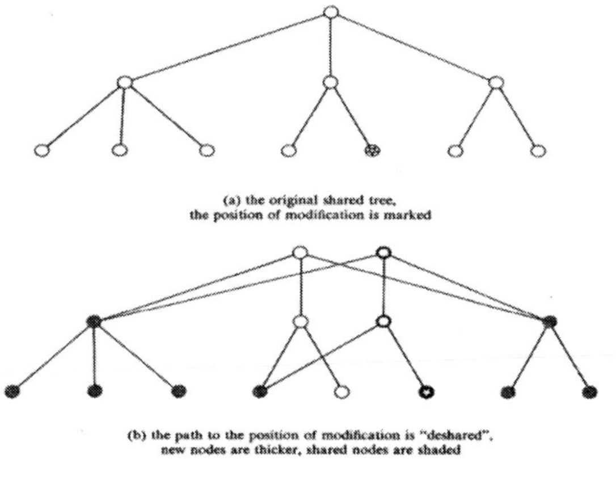

Figure 1. Updating a B-Tree (from[8])

Figure 2 shows how this approach affects the scenario of databases and transactions described in the Introduction.

Let us start with a database D initially synchronized with the data abase file. There will be data structures including a list of objects and a list of names, but we show just one in the illustration.

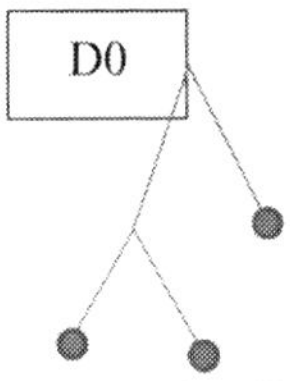

A transaction T starts by using the same data structures as the database.

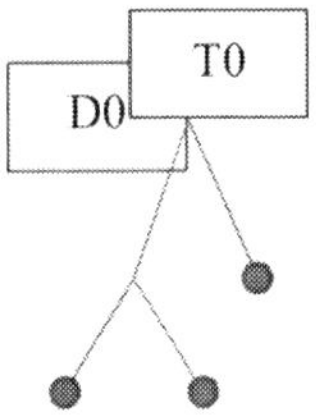

When the transaction makes a change, it creates new root nodes as required, but continues to share the rest of the data structures (indexes, lists of objects etc.).

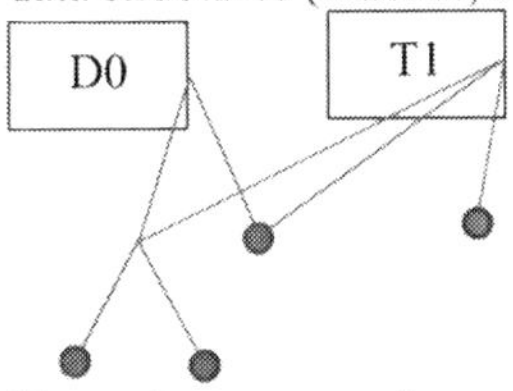

If another transaction commits in the meantime, the database will be replaced by a new one sharing the same data structures apart from the new root node.

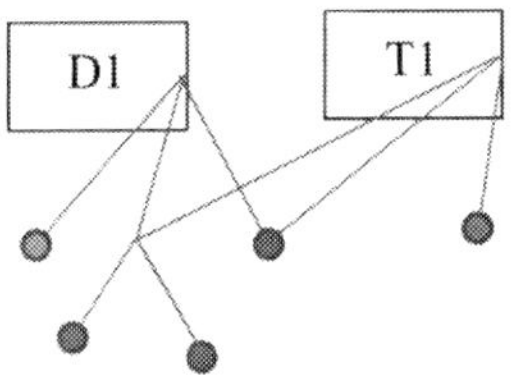

These changes do not affect the transaction's data structures.

When our transaction commits, (it can only do so after checking for no conflicts), its new information is added into the database's data structures, creating new root nodes as required.

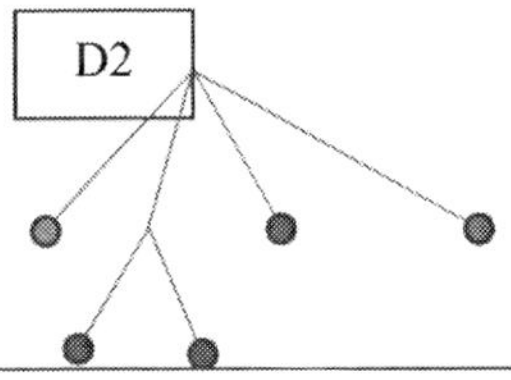

Figure 2. Shareable data structures and transaction behaviour

Care is needed when shareable data structures are used inside mutable structures. If such an unsafe object A contains an immutable dictionary d, then we need to remember to write

lock(A) d += (k,v); in Java we use a synchronized block **synchronized**(A) { d = d.add(k,v); }. The only place StrongDBMS finds it necessary to use such locking is for the global list of databases. File and stream objects are also locked when required to facilitate operating system interactions

The memory allocator must work harder with shareable data structures, but in complex software, this happens anyway, and if arrays are used, a lot of time is spent in copying.

B. Bookmarks instead of Enumerators

Both C# and Java always use Enumerators or Iterators in the standard libraries [9][10]. For an enumerator E, one moves to the next item in a collection using E.MoveNext(). This is obviously unsafe even for an immutable collection, as E might have been passed in as a parameter or copied somewhere else. In this work, we exclusively use Bookmarks for our shareable collections.

For any shareable collection as defined here, there is a method called First() that returns a bookmark to the first entry of the collection (First() returns null if the collection is empty). And given any Bookmark B, we get a bookmark to the next entry if any by B = B.Next().

Neither language provides us with a useful syntax for iteration using bookmarks, but it is easy to get used to writing

for (**var** b=C.First(); b!=**null**; b=b.Next())

Bookmarks iterate through the list as it stood when the First() bookmark was created. It is very convenient to be allowed to modify the list as it is being traversed. (The standard libraries do not allow mutable List structures to be modified during iteration.)

III. Architecture of the DBMS

The design goals mentioned at the start of Section I almost dictate some important features of the DBMS architecture. Each element of the binary API should be serializable, for transport from the client to the server and for serialization to the transaction log as persistent database objects. Some of the serializable objects represent SQL constructs, translated from SQL into this form in the client library. Each database object has a readonly uid field consisting of its immutable file position on disk.

A. Permanent uids for database objects

A file position will not be known until it is committed (serialized) to disk, and so because of the readonly nature of the uid, the commit will be done inside a constructor. In this section we will use C# for the code illustrations (the Java code is similar and can be reviewed in [4]):

```
protected    SDbObject(SDbObject    s,    AStream    f)
:base(s.type)
{
    uid = f.Length;
    f.uids = f.uids + (s.uid, uid);
    f.WriteByte((byte)s.type);
}
```

In this fragment, we can see the uid being set as the current file length before we write the first byte (the type) of the SDbObject subclass. We also see a dictionary called uids maintained by the file stream structure f, which associates the previous unique identifier with the new permanent uid.

The next step in the design is to decide what the previous uid was. This is assigned at the time the SDbObject is created for addition to the transaction. The transaction maintains a private sequence of uids for its SDbObjects. When the SdbObject is created for the transaction we have:

```
protected SDbObject(Types t,STransaction tr) :base(t)
{
   uid = tr.uid+1;
}
```

Objects such as table or column references arriving from the client may have uids assigned by the client-side parser if the names alone would be ambiguous. Because of separation of concerns between client and server, the client does not interpret these (for example, it will not know what columns are defined for a table). This is an important point since any schema information held in the client will, in general, be out of date.

B. Database

The database knows what its schema objects are, indexed by their permanent uids, and has a name catalogue for top-level objects such as base tables.

The first constructor for a database (cold start) gives the name and initializes the other information:

```
SDatabase(string fname)
{
   name = fname;
   objects = SDict<long, SDbObject>.Empty;
   names = SDict<string, SDbObject>.Empty;
   curpos = 0;
}
```

If there is a database file on disk, it is loaded into memory, deserializing its contents from the file and installing them in the database structure. We see some examples of this process below.

Creating a copy of the database is just:

```
protected SDatabase(SDatabase db)
{
   name = db.name;
   objects = db.objects;
   names = db.names;
   curpos = db.curpos;
}
```

We see that copying (taking a snapshot of) a database costs almost nothing (just four pointers).

The database structure is immutable so that any update requires the construction of a new instance. The database structure has a constructor that updates its dictionaries of schema objects in a new instance:

```
protected virtual SDatabase New(SDict<long,SDbObject>
     o, SDict<string,SDbObject> ns, long c)
{
    return new SDatabase(this, o, ns, c);
}
```

The current database (this) is made available to the constructor so that other data pointers (in this case, just the database name) that have not been changed can be copied into the new object. Here is the constructor:

```
protected SDatabase(SDatabase db, SDict<long,
SDbObject> obs, SDict<string,SDbObject> nms, long c)
{
   name = db.name;
   objects = obs;
   names = nms;
   curpos = c;
}
```

C. Installing database objects

The method in the database class for installing a table, e.g., when loading the database on startup, is very simple – of course it returns a new database object using the New method given above:

```
public SDatabase Install(STable t, long c)
{
  return New(objects+(t.uid, t),names+(t.name, t), c);
}
```

Tables maintain their own readonly lists of columns, rows and indexes, so installing a column creates a new version of the table object as well as a new database:

```
public SDatabase Install(SColumn c, long p)
{
  var obs = objects;
  if (c.uid >= STransaction._uid)
      obs += (c.uid, c);
  var tb = ((STable)obs[c.table])+c;
  return New(obs+(c.table,tb), names+(tb.name,tb), p);
}
```

It is important that very little data copying is required to make a new table object: it contains merely a small set of references to the roots of tree structures, some of which will have been updated.

The database does not directly include columns in its list of objects (but transactions do, as described below). There is a global static mutable collection of file streams with exclusive access to the databases currently open on the server, and a database looks up the appropriate file and locks it when it needs to access the disk.

Records, updates and deletes do not need to be in these memory structures as they can be retrieved from the disk file when required (However, if a lot of clients use the same database, the saving in memory is at the cost of increased contention on the file stream. An object cache would also be worth considering).

D. Transaction

We make STransaction a subclass of SDatabase so that it inherits the immutable information from the database on creation, including the current file position of the database (c in the above New method) at the start of the transaction. The code for starting a transaction is just a constructor:

```
public STransaction(SDatabase d,bool auto) :base(d)
{
   autoCommit = auto;
   rollback = d._Rollback;
   uid = _uid;
   readConstraints = SDict<long, bool>.Empty;
}
```

The code called for the base constructor is just the code for copying a Database, shown earlier.

Objects proposed for addition in the transaction (including records, updates and deletes) are added to the transaction's objects using its private sequence of uids, and this sequence is traversed on commit. (Recall that transactions cannot see other transactions so their sequences of uids are separate.)

In order to support long transactions, we recall that schema objects and records defined in a transaction should be usable in the transaction, so the transaction needs to install them in the dictionaries and indexes it has inherited from the database. It uses the same install code as the database, but with its own version of the New method that creates a transaction object instead of a database object.

When the transaction commits, the transaction's objects are installed in the database, and the transaction object can be forgotten.

E. Detection of transaction conflicts

The Commit method for the transaction object needs to consider whether conflicting changes may have occurred in the database before a commit can be agreed. As mentioned above, the transaction already has the file position at the start of the transaction. The transaction now looks at the current state of the file: if objects have been added by other transactions, it compares with the changes to be committed. If there are conflicts or anything read by the transaction has been modified, the commit cannot proceed, and a transaction conflict exception will be raised. If all is well, the database file is locked, and the process is repeated for any commits that may have happened before the lock. If there are still no conflicts, as the file is already locked the transaction's objects can be committed to the database using the mechanism described at the start of subsection A above. These installation steps result in a new database object, which is then installed in the server's static mutable list of databases:

```
public static void Install(SDatabase db)
{
    lock(files) databases = databases+(db.name, db);
}
```

The database file is then unlocked.

F. Query processing and RowSets

StrongDBMS follows the SQL standard closely except that it allows case-sensitive identifiers and a small set of primitive data types. Full details are in [5], but some example SQL statements may help:

```
create table Voc (Id integer, Word string, Notes string)
insert Voc values (1,'a','Indefinite article')
select from Voc where Word>'Z'
```

As mentioned above, parsing of SQL queries is done on the client, so that the client sends the server a Serialisable object such as an SQuery or an SInsertStatement. As the server receives these, there is a *Lookup* method to identify the columns and tables referred to by name, and construct versions of the received object where the object references are to the correct schema objects.

The next step is that a RowSet is constructed for the results of the query or the data for the insert or other command. In the presence of subqueries or grouping, etc., this process may be recursive, so that the query's RowSet method supplies a stack called Context in which the current values of selectors can be found. The RowSet contains a copy of the transaction that has the readConstraints list populated during this recursion.

RowSets are traversed using a special subclass of Bookmark (RowBookmark), which holds a row object for the current row of the traversal, and a base table record if this is a row of a base table. In general, the selectors in the query can be expression objects, so that for returning results to the client, the selector expressions use the same Lookup method to compute the results, using new Context extended by the current RowBookmark.

The RowSet method recursively constructs row sets for traversing tables in joins and subqueries, for applying an ordering or a search condition and for evaluating aggregations. For join processing the row sets participating in the join are first ordered using the columns specified in the join-condition or implied by a natural join.

The final traversal for the client serializes the results using Json format. Non-query client requests that use RowSets include insert, update and delete statements for base tables, and these use the records referred to in the RowBookmark.

G. Transaction Programming Paradigm

As described above, a transaction in StrongDBMS operates on the database as if it were private since the start of the transaction. This isolation provides true conflict serializability [11], which is strictly stronger than that required by the ISO SQL standard [12]. The private transaction context allows a straight-forward programming for the transaction logic without concern on lock timeouts or concurrency conflicts before the COMMIT. Further details on the isolation model are given in Chapter 1 section "Concurrency Control" in [3].

IV. BENCHMARKING STRONGDBMS

A. Parameter tuning

As suggested above, StrongDBMS adopts a standard data format for the database file that is independent of locale or machine architecture. Within the server it is obvious that standard **int** and **long** data types will be used for integers where possible and a multibyte alternative for big integers.

It is less obvious how to fine-tune the size of B-Tree "buckets". B-Trees have a fixed bucket size N, and then allow nodes other than the root to have between N and 2N (or 2N+1) child nodes. Experimentally it can be established that performance is independent of the value of N over the range 6 to 32. Currently StrongDBMS uses N=8. With smaller values of N there are more nodes and deeper trees, while if N is larger the cost of copying bucket contents becomes more significant.

B. Performance Benchmarks

Relational DBMS traditionally use the Transaction Processing Council's TPC/C benchmark [13] which models a 1980s-style Online Transaction Processing application. An interesting measure is provided by the New Order transaction, which models a clerk filling in a warehouse order for a customer. Each warehouse serves ten districts, each with 3000 customers, and 100000 products. An order may have up to 20 lines, each a given quantity of a specific product identified by its code. As the clerk enters the fields on the form the database supplies details: the customer's name and address, the customer's discount, orders to date, etc., and for each line of the order supplies the product description and price, updates the current stock level, and computes the total cost per line and per order. On completion of the order the transaction is committed. Each order takes dozens of server round-trips.

On a personal computer, an implementation following the details prescribed by TPC typically will execute about 20 New Order transactions per second. The initial state of the database on Strong occupies 100MB. In Table 1, this initial database file has already been constructed (it was excessively slow to recreate in the Java on Linux configuration), and timings were taken for the initialization of the system (cold start) and for 2000 New Order transactions. The client and hardware were the same for all four tests (Intel i5 processor, 16 GB of memory).

TABLE I. TPC/C 2000 NEW ORDER TRANSACTIONS

Server Implementation	Operating System	Cold start	2000 New Orders
C# 8.0	Windows 10	16 sec	48 sec
C#	Debian 9 (mono)	10 sec	79 sec
Java 11 (32 bit)	Windows 10	7 sec	51 sec
Java 11 (32 bit)	Debian 9 (mono)	6 sec	242 sec

V. CONCLUSIONS

This paper has introduced StrongDBMS, a new database management system based on the ideas of append-only transactions log-file and shareable data structures. Together they provide the capabilities of transaction isolation, durability, atomicity and consistency. This paper presented the design rationale and trade-off for the StrongDBMS approach. StrongDBMS has been co-developed in Java and C#, and will continue to be supported in both programming languages. As mentioned above, StrongDBMS is still under development. The current state has enabled us to envision and discuss the benefits and limitations of the approach. The design of StrongDBMS is intended to support multithreading, so that the server handles each transaction in a different thread, and threads sharing a database use the database file for synchronization when a commit is requested. Our next steps will include tests for verifying performance with multithreading.

We have presented how the current implementation of StrongDBMS performs in the Transaction Processing Council's TPC/C benchmark.

ACKNOWLEDGMENTS

It is a pleasure to acknowledge the inspiration, encouragement and contributions of members of the DBTech community and from Stephen Hegner.

REFERENCES

[1] M. K. Crowe, "Transactions in the Pyrrho Database Engine. in Databases and Applications" [ed.] M H Hamza. Innsbruck, Austria : ACTA Press, 2005. pp. 71-76.

[2] A. Fekete, D. Liarokapis, E. J. O'Neil, P. E. O'Neil, and D. E. Shasha, "Making snapshot isolation serializable", ACM Transactions on Database Systems, 30:2. 2005 pp. 429-528.

[3] M. Laiho, M. Kurki, M. Crowe, F. Laux, D. Dervos, and K. Hirvonen, Introduction to Transaction Programming: DBTechNet.org, [Online] 2019. dbtechnet.org/papers/IntroToTransactionProgramming.pdf.

[4] M. Crowe, C. Begg, F. Laux, and M. Laiho, "Data Validation for Big Live Data. Barcelona" : DBKDA 2017, The Ninth International Conference on Advances in Databases, Knowledge and Data Applications, 2017, pp.30-36.

[5] M. Crowe, "Shareable Data Structures". GitHub. [retrieved: March, 2019] https://github.com/MalcolmCrowe/ShareableDataStructures.

[6] M. Ardis, D. Budgen, G. W. Hislop, J. Offutt, M. Sebern, and W. Visser, SE 2014: "Curriculum Guidelines for Undergraduate Degree Programs in Software Engineering", Long Beach, CA : 2015, Computer, Vol. 48 (11), pp. 106-109.

[7] B. P. Shults, "Teaching Data Structures: thread safety and components". Boston, MA : IEEE, 2002. 32nd Annual Frontiers in Education.

[8] T. Krijnen, and G. L. T. Meertens, "Making B-Trees work for B". Amsterdam: Stichting Mathematisch Centrum, 1982, Technical Report IW 219/83.

[9] Microsoft. System. Collections. Immutable. 2015 www.nuget.org [retrieved: March, 2019].

[10] Oracle. Java Collections Framework.

[11] H. Berenson, J. Gray, J. Melton, E. J. O'Neill, and P. E. O'Neill, "A Critique of ANSI SQL Isolation Levels". San Jose, CA: ACM. Proceedings of the 1995 ACM SIGMOD International Conference. 1995. pp. 1-10.

[12] J. Melton, Information Technology - Database Languages - SQL : ISO/IEC, 2016. 9075.

[13] Transaction Processing Council. [retrieved: March, 2019]. http://www.tpc.org.

A Denormalization Approach to Answering Join Queries

Mohammed Hamdi[1], Kavya Narne[2], Hamzah Arishi[3], Feng Yu[4], and Wen-Chi Hou[2]
[1]Department of Computer Science, Najran University,
Najran, Saudi Arabia
E-mail: mahamdi@nu.edu.sa
[2]Department of Computer Science, Southern Illinois University,
Carbondale, IL, USA
E-mail:{kavya, hou}@cs.siu.edu
[3]College of Commuting and Informatics, Saudi Electronic University
Riyadh, Saudi Arabia
E-mail: a.hamzah@seu.edu.sa
[4]Department of Computer Science and Information Systems
Youngstown State University
Youngstown, OH, USA
E-mail: fyu@ysu.edu

Abstract— **Relational databases may not be an efficient solution to store highly connected data. Graph traversals over high-connected data require complex join operations. These join operations are generally very expensive and hard to compute. In the light of this, a data structure, called Join Core is emerging. Join Core pre-stores equi-join relationships of tuples on inexpensive and space abundant devices, such as disks, to facilitate query processing. The equi-join relationships are captured, grouped, and stored as various tables on disks. This methodology assists the join queries to be answered quickly by merely merging these tables without having to perform expensive joins. We use Join Core and Neo4j graph database in our experiments as they deal with highly connected data. Experiments are performed to compare the query processing time and space consumptions between them. Preliminary experimental results showed that Join Core outperforms Neo4j when complex queries are processed.**

Keywords—Query Processing; Join Queries; Graph Databases; Equi-Join.

I. INTRODUCTION

In many applications, such as Semantic Web, Social and Computer Networks, and in Geographic Applications, data are highly connected and have a natural representation as a graph. In these contexts, relational databases may not be suitable for those highly connected data where data are spread among relations, and it is hard to capture and group the join relationships among data over traditional systems [24]. Moreover, graph traversals over high-connected data involve complex join operations [7][24]. These join operations are generally very expensive and hard to compute. Complex queries involving multiple joins of large relations can easily take minutes or even hours to compute over the target database. For the above reasons, we previously proposed an anti-relational approach, called Join Core in [22].

Here, the paper extends the work of Join Core in [22] and makes the following contribution:

- Detailed discussions on answering cyclic join queries, and queries with other joins.
- We analyze the time and space consumption of using Join Core.
- We propose effective methods that can significantly reduce the space consumption of the Join Core.
- We implement the Join Core and perform experiments to compare its performance efficiency with a Neo4j graph database instead of MySQL.

The technique can ease the job of the query optimizer because there are fewer or no joins to perform and provide less resources consumptions, e.g., Central Processing Unit (CPU) and memory. A number of experiments have been done to compare the performance of Join Core and Neo4j [24]. The experimental results show that processing queries with Join Core is faster than with Neo4j. This is because there is no need to perform join operations at run time with Join Core while in Neo4j, the path traversal operations depend upon the complexities of the relationships of tuples. We believe the benefits of Join Core, namely instant responses, fast query processing, and small memory consumptions, are well worth the additional storage space incurred.

The rest of the paper is organized as follows. Section II surveys work in materialized views and Section III introduces the terminology. Section IV shows a sample Join Core and how it can be used to answer equi-join queries. Section V lays down the theoretical foundation for answering equi-join queries using the Join Core. Section VI extends the framework to queries with other types of joins and set operations. Section VII analyzes the time and space consumptions of the Join Core, and discusses measures to reduce the space consumption. Section VII reports experimental results. Finally, conclusions are presented in Section VIII.

II. LITERATURE SURVEY

In this section, we discuss briefly the literature survey. Materialized views, join indices, and graph databases are related to our work as both attempt to pre-compute data to facilitate query processing.

Materialized views generally focus on Select-Project-Join (SPJ) queries and, perhaps, on final grouping and aggregate functions. The select and project operations in the views confine and complicate the uses of the views. As a result, much research has focused on how to select the most beneficial views to materialize [8][10][15][19] and how to choose an appropriate set of materialized views to answer a query [1][9][16].

Materialized views materialize selected query results, while Join Core materializes selected equi-join relationships. Therefore, materialized views may benefit queries that are relevant to the selected queries, while Join Core can benefit queries that are related to the selected equi-join relationships, which include queries with arbitrary sequences of equi-, semi-, outer-, anti-joins and set operators.

A join index [14][21] for a join stores the equi-join result in a concise manner as pairs of identifiers of tuples that would match in the join operation. It has been shown that joins can be performed more efficiently with join indices than the traditional join algorithms. However, it still requires at least one scan of the operand relations, writes and reads of temporary files (as large as the source relations), and generating intermediate result relations (for queries with more than one join). On the other hand, with Join Core, join results are readily available without accessing any source or intermediate relation. Very little memory and computations are required. In addition, join indices are not useful to other join operators, such as outer-joins and anti-joins.

Graph databases use the graph data model to structure and perform the main database systems operations (Create, Read, Update, and Delete). The graph data model has two basic elements: node and relationship. Unlike the relational databases, the graph databases store the relationships as entities which make it more flexible and scalable. This is because when the data model expands or business requirement changes, it is easier to add connection (relationship) between entities [7][24].

Graph databases also use the graph model to pre-store the join relationships of tuples and query connections at creation time and make them readily available for any later join query operation [24]. This can result in no penalties for complex join queries at runtime as the Join Core does. They use the index- free so that the query processing time depends on the searched graph length rather than the total size of the graph. However, the path traversal operations in the complex relationships of nodes sometimes decelerate the query processing time. In contrast, the result size of the query, not the complexity of join query determines the query processing time with Join Core.

III. TERMINOLOGY

In this paper, we assume all the data model and queries are based on the set semantics. The equi-join operator is the most commonly used operator to combine data spread across relations. Other useful joins, such as the semi-join, outer-join, and anti-join, are all related to the equi-join. Therefore, we shall first lay down the theoretical foundation of Join Core based on the equi-join, and then extend the framework to other joins in Section VI. Hereafter, we shall use, for simplicity, a join for an equi-join, unless otherwise stated.

A join graph is commonly used to describe the equi-join relationships between pairs of relations. These relationships are generally defined before the database has been created. Certainly, one can also include other frequently referenced ad-hoc equi-join relationships in the graph.

For simplicity, we assume there is at most one equi-join relationship between each pair of relations.

Definition 1. (Join Graph of a Database). Let D be a database with n relations $R_1, R_2, \ldots, R_n$, and $G(V, E)$ be the join graph of D, where V is a set of nodes that represents the set of relations in D, i.e., $V = \{R_1, R_2, R_3, \ldots, R_n\}$, and $E = \{(R_i, R_j) \mid R_i, R_j \in V, i \neq j)\}$, is a set of edges, in which each represents an equi-join relationship that has been defined between R_i and R_j, $i \neq j$.s

If the join graph is not connected, one can consider each connected component separately. Therefore, we shall assume all join graphs are connected.

Each join comes with a predicate, omitted in the graph, specifying the requirements that a result tuple of the join must satisfy, e.g., $R_1.attr1 = R_2.attr2$. For simplicity, we shall use a join, a join edge, and a join predicate interchangeably. We also assume all relations and join edges are numbered.

Example 1. (*Join Graph*). Figure. 1(a) shows the join graph of a database with five relations R_1, R_2, R_3, R_4, and R_5, connected by join edges, numbered from 6 to 9.

To round out the theoretical framework, we shall introduce a concept, called the *trivial equi-join*. Each tuple in a relation R_i can be considered as a result tuple of a trivial join between R_i and itself with a join predicate $R_i.key = R_i.key$, where *key* is the (set of) key attribute(s) of R_i. Trivial join predicates are not shown explicitly in the join graphs. All join edges in Figure. 1(a), such as 6, 7, 8, and 9, are non-trivial or regular joins.

We have reserved predicate number i, $1 \leq i \leq 5$, for trivial join predicate i, which is automatically satisfied by every tuple in relation R_i. The concept of trivial join predicates will be useful later when we discuss a query that contains outer-joins, anti-joins, or no joins. Hereafter, all joins and join predicates refer to non-trivial ones, unless otherwise stated.

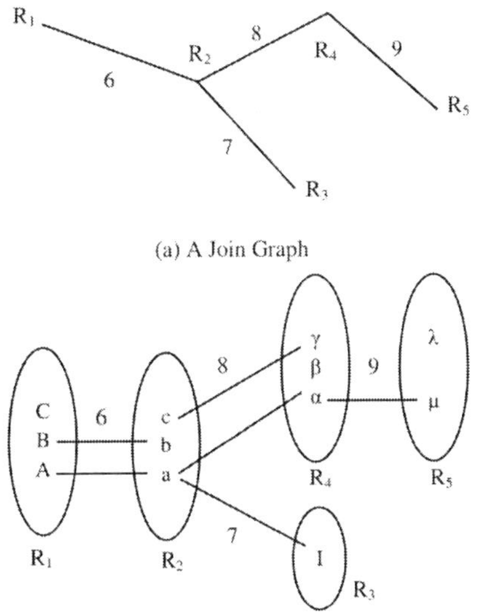

(a) A Join Graph

(b) Matching of Join Attribute Values

Figure 1. A Join Graph and Matching Tuples

To conserve space, a database and its join graph refer to only the parts of the database and join graphs that are of our interest and for which we intend to build Join Cores. We will discuss other space conservation measures in Section VII.

Definition 2. (Join Queries). Let $\bowtie(\{R_i, \ldots, R_j\}, E')$ be a join query, representing joins of the set of relations $\{R_i, \ldots, R_j\} \subseteq V$, $1 \leq i, \ldots, j \leq n$, with respect to the set of join predicates $E' \subseteq E$ among them.

Definition 3. (Join Graph of a Join Query). The join graph of a join query $\bowtie(\{R_i, \ldots, R_j\}, E')$, denoted by $G'(V', E')$, is a connected subgraph of $G(V, E)$, where $V' = \{R_i, \ldots, R_j\} \subseteq V$, and $E' \subseteq E$ is the set of join predicates specified in the query.

The join graph of a join query is also called *a query graph*. We shall exclude queries that must execute Cartesian products or θ-joins, where $\theta \neq$ "=", from discussion as Join Core cannot facilitate executions of such operators.

Example 2. (*Matching of Join Attribute Values*). Figure. 1(b) shows the matching of join attribute values between tuples. Tuples are represented by their IDs in the Figure. That is, R_1 has 3 tuples, A, B, C, i.e., $R_1 = \{A, B, C\}$. $R_2 = \{a, b, c\}$, $R_3 = \{I\}$, $R_4 = \{\alpha, \beta, \gamma\}$, $R_5 = \{\mu, \lambda\}$.

The edges between tuples represent matches of join attribute values. For example, tuples A and B of R_1 match tuples a and b of R_2, respectively. Tuple a has two other matches, I of R_3 and α of R_4. c of R_2 matches γ of R_4, and α matches μ of R_5.

Definition 4. ((Maximally) Extended Match Tuple). Given a database $D = \{R_1, \ldots, R_n\}$ and its join graph G, an extended match tuple $(t_k, \ldots, t_l)$, where $1 \leq k, \ldots, l \leq n$, $t_k \in R_k$, $\ldots$, $t_l \in R_l$, and $R_k, \ldots, R_l$ are all distinct relations, represents a set of tuples $\{t_k, \ldots, t_l\}$ that generates a result tuple in $\{t_k\} \bowtie \ldots \bowtie \{t_l\}$. A maximally extended match tuple $(t_k, \ldots, t_l)$, is an extended match tuple if no tuple t_m in R_m ($\notin \{R_k, \ldots, R_l\}$) matches any of the tuples $t_k, \ldots, t_l$ in join attribute values.

It can be observed that in Figure. 1(b), (A, a, I, α, μ) is a maximally extended match tuple. The same can be said of (B, b) because the match cannot be extended by any tuple in relations other than R_1 and R_2. Similarly, (c, γ), as well as (C), (β), and (λ), is also a maximally extended match tuple.

IV. JOIN CORE STRUCTURE AND CONSTRUCTION

In this section, we show an example of a Join Core and explain how it is structured and used to answer equi-join queries.

A. Join Core Structure and Naming

Consider Figure. 1 again. The join relationships we wish to store are (A, a, I, α, μ), (B, b), (c, γ), (C), (β), and (λ), each representing a maximally extended match tuple. We intend to store these maximally extended match tuples in various tables based on the join predicates, both trivial and non-trivial ones, they satisfy. These tables form the *Join Core*.

Example 3. (*Sample Join Core*). Figure. 2 shows the Join Core for the database in Figure. 1. The attributes of the Join Core tables, i.e., 1, 2, 3, 4, and 5, represent the sets of (interesting) attributes of R_1, R_2, R_3, R_4, and R_5, respectively, and are called the R_1, R_2, …, R_5 components of the tables.

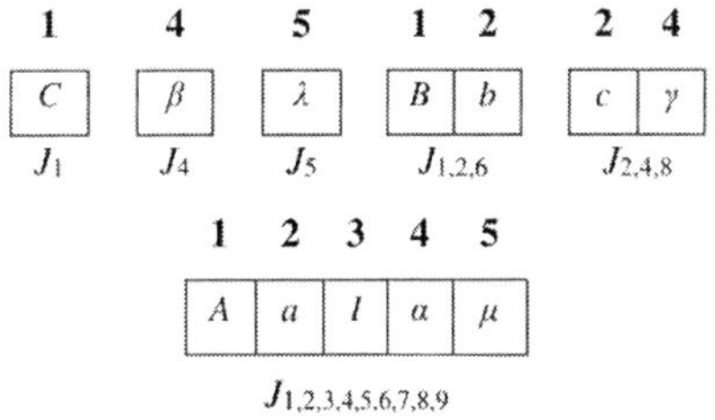

Figure 2. Join Core

(B, b) is stored in $J_{1,2,6}$ because (B, b) satisfies join predicate 6, and trivial predicates 1 ($B \in R_1$) and 2 ($b \in R_2$). Similarly, (c, γ) is stored in $J_{2,4,8}$ and (A, a, I, α, μ) is stored in $J_{1,2,3,4,5,6,7,8,9}$. C ($\in R_1$), β ($\in R_4$), and λ ($\in R_5$) satisfy only trivial predicates and thus are stored in J_1, J_4, and J_5, respectively.

Assume join predicate numbers 1, …, n are reserved for trivial joins between R_1, …, R_n and themselves, respectively, and non-trivial predicates are numbered from n+1 to n+e, where e is the number of join edges in the join graph.

Definition 5. (Join Core). A join Core is composed of a set of tables $J_{k, \ldots, l}$, $1 \leq k, \ldots, l \leq n+e$, each of which stores a set of maximally extended match tuples that satisfy *all and only* the join predicates k, …, l. Each table $J_{k, \ldots, l}$ is called a *Join*

Core table (or *relation*). The indices $k, \ldots l$ of the table $J_{k, \ldots, l}$ is called the name of the table for convenience.

For simplicity, we shall call a maximally extended match tuple in a Join Core table a match tuple, to be differentiated from a tuple in a regular relation.

B. Answering Queries using Join Core

The name of a Join Core table specifies the join predicates satisfied by the match tuples stored in it. On the other hand, a join query specifies predicates that must be satisfied by the result tuples. Therefore, to answer a query is to look for Join Core tables whose names contain the predicates of the query.

Consider Figure.1 and 2 and the query $\bowtie(\{R_1, R_2, R_3, R_4, R_5\}, \{6, 7, 8, 9\})$. The components of the result tuples must satisfy predicates 6, 7, 8, and 9. In addition, the components themselves also satisfy trivial predicates 1, 2, 3, 4, 5. Thus, we look for Join Core tables whose names contain predicates 1, 2, 3, 4, 5, 6, 7, 8, and 9. That is, $\bowtie(\{R_1, R_2, R_3, R_4, R_5\}, \{6, 7, 8, 9\}) = J_{1,2,3,4,5,6,7,8,9}$.

As for $\bowtie(\{R_1, R_2\}, \{6\})$, while $J_{1,2,6}$ certainly contains some result tuples, $J_{1,2,3,4,5,6,7,8,9}$ also contains some result tuples because tuples in $J_{1,2,3,4,5,6,7,8,9}$ also satisfy 1, 2, and 6. That is, $\bowtie(\{R_1, R_2\}, \{6\}) = \pi_{1,2}(J_{1,2,6}) \cup \pi_{1,2}(J_{1,2,3,4,5,6,7,8,9})$. Similarly, $\bowtie(\{R_2, R_4\}, \{8\}) = \pi_{2,4}(J_{2,4,8}) \cup \pi_{2,4}(J_{1,2,3,4,5,6,7,8,9})$; $\bowtie(\{R_2, R_3\}, \{7\}) = \pi_{2,3}(J_{1,2,3,4,5,6,7,8,9})$.

It even holds for queries containing no non-trivial joins. For example, $R_1 = \pi_1 J_1 \cup \pi_1(J_{1,2,6}) \cup \pi_1(J_{1,2,3,4,5,6,7,8,9})$, $R_2 = \pi_2(J_{1,2,6}) \cup \pi_2(J_{2,4,8}) \cup \pi_2(J_{1,2,3,4,5,6,7,8,9})$, $R_3 = \pi_3(J_{1,2,3,4,5,6,7,8,9})$, $R_4 = \pi_4 J_4 \cup \pi_4(J_{2,4,8}) \cup \pi_4(J_{1,2,3,4,5,6,7,8,9})$, and $R_5 = \pi_5 J_5 \cup \pi_5(J_{1,2,3,4,5,6,7,8,9})$. It is observed that R_i can be reconstructed from the Join Core, which implies that a Join Core can itself be the database, if one wishes to not store the relations in traditional ways.

Notice that when a non-trivial join predicate, such as 6, is satisfied by a match tuple, the associated trivial predicates on its operand relations, i.e., 1 and 2, are also satisfied automatically. Therefore, there is no need to match the trivial predicates of a query with the Join Core table names. That is, given a join query with a non-empty set of predicates $\{u, \ldots, v\}$, the result tuples can be found in Join Core tables whose names contain $u, \ldots, v$, without regard to trivial predicates. Trivial predicates cannot be ignored when a query contains no non-trivial joins, such as those described above or contains outer- or anti-joins, discussed later.

Duplicates need not be eliminated in individual $\pi_{i, \ldots, j}(J_{k, \ldots, l})$ above; they can be eliminated all at once when match tuples are merged in the final union operations. To identify duplicate result tuples, a simple hashing scheme is sufficient. Note that this is the only place that requires major memory consumption (in building a hash table).

The database system can begin to generate result tuples once the first block of a relevant Join Core table is read into memory, that is, instantly. The total computation time is also drastically reduced because there are no (or fewer) joins to perform.

C. Join Core Construction

Now, let us discuss how to construct a Join Core for a database. Tuples that find no match in one join may find matches in another join. For example, b finds no match in $R_2 \bowtie R_3$, but finds a match B in $R_1 \bowtie R_2$. Unfortunately, such join relationships can be lost in successive joins, for example, in $(R_1 \bowtie R_2) \bowtie R_3$.

Full outer-joins, or simply outer-joins, retain matching tuples as well as dangling tuples, and thus can capture all the join relationships. Any graph traversal method can be used here as long as it incurs no Cartesian products during the traversal.

For illustrative purpose, we assume a breadth-first traversal is adopted here. Relations are numbered based on the order encountered in the traversal. An outer-join is performed for each join edge. The output of the previous outer-join is used as an input to the next outer-join. The result tuples are distributed to Join Core tables based on the join predicates, both trivial and non-trivial ones, they have satisfied in the traversal.

Example 4. (Join Core Construction). Assume a breadth-first traversal of the join graph (Figure. 1(a)) from R_1 is performed. An outer-join is first performed between R_1 and R_2. It generates (intermediate) result tuples (A, a), (B, b), $(C, \text{-})$, and $(\text{-}, c)$. The next outer-join with R_3 generates (A, a, I), $(B, b, \text{-})$, $(C, \text{-}, \text{-})$ and $(\text{-}, c, \text{-})$. Then, the outer-join with R_4 generates (A, a, I, α), $(B, b, \text{-}, \text{-})$, $(C, \text{-}, \text{-}, \text{-})$, $(\text{-}, c, \text{-}, \gamma)$, and $(\text{-}, \text{-}, \text{-}, \beta)$. The final outer-join with R_5 generates (A, a, I, α, μ), $(B, b, \text{-}, \text{-}, \text{-})$, $(C, \text{-}, \text{-}, \text{-}, \text{-})$, $(\text{-}, c, \text{-}, \gamma, \text{-})$, $(\text{-}, \text{-}, \text{-}, \beta, \text{-})$, and $(\text{-}, \text{-}, \text{-}, \text{-}, \lambda)$, which are written, without nulls, to $J_{1,2,3,4,5,6,7,8,9}$, $J_{1,2,6}$, J_1, $J_{2,4,8}$, J_4, and J_5, respectively, based on the join predicates they satisfy.

V. ANSWERING EQUI-JOIN QUERIES

In this section, we formally discuss how a join query can be answered using the Join Core. First, we consider databases with acyclic join graphs, followed by databases with cyclic join graphs.

A. Acyclic Join Graph

As illustrated in the previous section, join queries with acyclic join graphs can be answered by simply extracting the requested components from Join Core tables whose names contain the join predicates specified in the queries.

Theorem 1. Let $\bowtie(\{R_i, \ldots, R_j\}, \{u, \ldots, v\})$ be joins of the set of relations $\{R_i, \ldots, R_j\}$ with respect to a set of join predicates $\{u, \ldots, v\} \neq \emptyset$. Let e be the number of join edges in the join graph,

$\bowtie(\{R_i, \ldots, R_j\}, \{u, \ldots, v\}) = \cup_{\{k, \ldots, l\} \supseteq \{u, \ldots, v\}} \pi_{i, \ldots, j}(J_{k, \ldots, l})$ where $1 \leq i, \ldots, j \leq n$, $1 \leq k, \ldots, l, u, \ldots, v \leq n+e$.

Here, we shall call $\{k, \ldots, l\} \supseteq \{u, \ldots, v\}$ or equivalently, $k \in\{u, \ldots, v\} \wedge \ldots \wedge l \in\{u, \ldots, v\}$ shall be called *(table name) selection criteria*.

B. *Cyclic Join Graph*

Figure. 3(a) shows a cyclic join graph. When a relation is visited in a, for example, breadth-first traversal, its attributes are added to the resulting schema. In a cyclic join graph however, a node may be visited more than once. For example, R_4 is visited through edge $\langle R_2, R_4\rangle$ for the first time, and then through $\langle R_3, R_4\rangle$ for the second time when the cycle forms. To differentiate matches associated with different edges, we shall create two copies of R_4, named R_4 (the original name) and R_5 (the next available relation number). Note that this is effectively converting a cyclic graph into an acyclic one. We shall call all copies of R_4, i.e., R_4 and R_5, alias relations of R_4. Note that a *cycle-completing* relation, such as R_4, may replicate more than once if it completes more than one cycle in the traversal. Figure. 3(b) shows the converted graph.

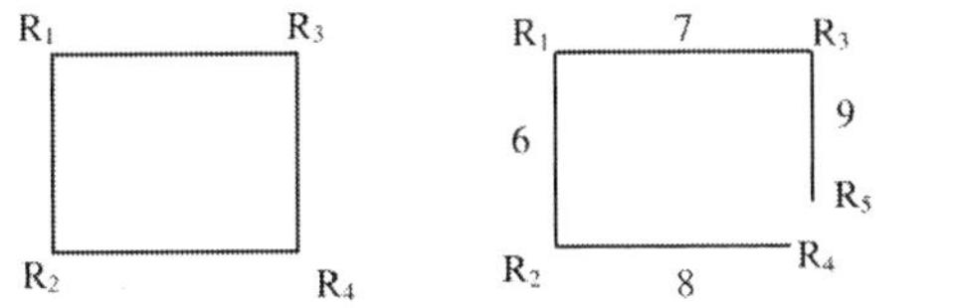

(a) A Cyclic Join Graph (b) A Converted Join Graph

Figure 3. Converting A Cyclic Graph

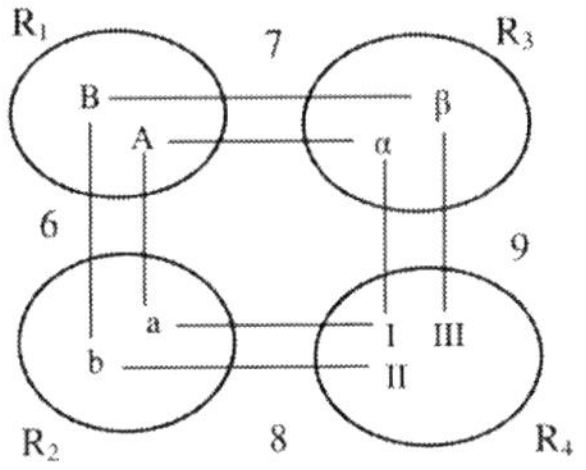

(a) Cyclic Join Relationship

1	2	3	4	5
A	*a*	*α*	*I*	*I*
B	*b*	*β*	*II*	*III*

$J_{1,2,3,4,5,6,7,8,9}$

(b) Join Core Tables

Figure 4. Cyclic Join Relationship and Join Core

With a cyclic join graph converted into an acyclic one, a Join Core can be constructed in the same way as before. However, to determine whether an extended match tuple contains a cycle or not, we need to check if the alias components have the same value.

Example 5. (Answering Cyclic Join Queries). Figure. 4 shows the join relationships and the Join Core for Figure 3. Consider a cyclic join query: $\bowtie(\{R_1, R_2, R_3, R_4\}, \{6, 7, 8, 9\})$. To ensure that it is the same tuple in the cycle-completing relation that satisfies both predicates 8 and 9, the alias components R_4 and R_5 must be the same. That is, a selection condition, $\sigma_{4=5}$, must be imposed. Thus, $\bowtie(\{R_1, R_2, R_3, R_4\}, \{6, 7, 8, 9\}) = \pi_{1,2,3,4}(\sigma_{4=5}(J_{1,2,3,4,5,6,7,8,9})) = \{(A, a, \alpha, I)\}$. On the other hand, (B, b, β, II, III) does not contain an answer to the query because its R_4 and R_5 components (i.e., II and III) are not the same.

Consequently, cycles in a query graph can be treated like ordinary acyclic join predicates, with the exception that additional constraints on the equalities of alias components must be added.

Theorem 2. Let $\bowtie(\{R_i, \ldots, R_j\}, \{u, \ldots, v\})$, $1 \leq i, \ldots, j \leq n$, be a query contains cycles.
$\bowtie(\{R_i, \ldots, R_j\}, \{u, \ldots, v\}) = \cup_{\{k, \ldots, l\} \supseteq \{u, \ldots, v\}} \pi_{i, \ldots, j}(\sigma_F(J_{k,\ldots,l}))$

C. *Multiple Join Edges Between Relations*

It is possible that there is more than one join edge between a pair of relations. This situation can be easily resolved by treating it as a cycle.

Example 6. (Multiple Edges between Relations) Assume there are two join edges, e_1 and e_2, between R_1 and R_2. Then, one can pick any relation, say R_2, as the cycle completing relation, replicate it, and call the replica R_3. Finally, let e_1 be the edge between R_1 and R_2, and e_2 be the edge between R_1 and R_3.

VI. QUERIES WITH OTHER JOINS

Now, a join can be an equi-, semi-, outer- or anti-join. A join generates result tuples dependent upon whether the equi-join predicate between the operand relations are satisfied (in an equi- or semi-join) or not satisfied (in an anti-join). A little deliberation reveals that match tuples that do not satisfy an equi-join predicate can be found in Join Core tables whose names do not contain that predicate, recalling that Join Core table names specify *all and only* the equi-join predicates satisfied. An outer-join generates a result tuple no matter whether the equi-join predicate is satisfied or not.

A join query consisting of a sequence of join operators has a *query predicate* that is a logical combination of the individual predicates of constituent joins. We attempt to obtain query result tuples from Join Core tables whose names satisfy the query predicates. Here, we focus on how to formulate the query predicates as *(table name) selection criteria* for Join Core tables that contain the query result tuples. For example, satisfying predicate p is rewritten as $p \in \{k, \ldots, l\}$, where $\{k, \ldots, l\}$ is the set of indices of a Join Core table name.

Afterward, specific handlings, such as removal of unwanted attributes, equality checking for alias components (for cycle-completing relations), and padding null values for "missing" attributes (for outer-joins), are performed. For simplicity, we shall only briefly describe these afterward handlings.

A. *Single-Join Queries*

We start by deriving the selection criteria, denoted by S, for queries with only one join operator. Let p be the equi-join predicate between R_i and R_j. Consider R_i *op* R_j, where *op* is either an equi-join, semi-join, outer-join, or anti-join.

1) Equi-Join. As discussed, to compute $R_i \bowtie R_j$ with a join predicate p, we look for Join Core tables $J_{k,...,l}$ whose indices contain p, i.e., $S = p \in \{k, ..., l\}$. As mentioned, trivial predicates i and j need not, but can, be included in S because they are satisfied automatically and must have appeared as part of the names of the tables satisfying p.

2) Semi-Join. The left semi-join $R_i \ltimes R_j$ and right semi-join $R_i \rtimes R_j$ extract only the R_i and R_j components from $R_i \bowtie R_j$, respectively. Here, we shall not be concerned about the projection operations. Consequently, the selection criterion S for a semi-join is the same as that for an equi-join, that is, $S = p \in \{k, ..., l\}$.

3) Outer-Join. While computing $R_i ⟗ R_j$ during the construction of the Join Core, each pair of tuples satisfying predicate p forms an output tuple. In addition, each non-matching tuple from either R_i (satisfying the trivial predicate i) or R_j (satisfying the trivial predicate j) also forms an output tuple. Consequently, to answer the query $R_i ⟗ R_j$, we look for Join Core tables $J_{k,...,l}$ such that $(i \in \{k, ..., l\} \wedge (\neg (p \in \{k, ..., l\}))) \vee (j \in \{k, ..., l\} \wedge (\neg(p \in \{k, ..., l\}))) \vee p \in \{k, ..., l\}$, where $\neg$ is the logical "not" operator and $\vee$ is the logical "or" operator. Since $p \in \{k, ..., l\}$ implies $i \in \{k, ..., l\} \wedge j \in \{k, ..., l\}$, the selection criteria S can be simplified to $S = i \in \{k, ..., l\} \vee j \in \{k, ..., l\}$. Trivial predicates i and j cannot be omitted from S because no non-trivial predicates that reference i and j are satisfied.

A left outer-join $R_i ⟕ R_j$ asks for matching tuple pairs and non-matching tuples from R_i. Therefore, $S = i \in \{k, ..., l\}$. Similarly, for a right outer-join $R_i ⟖ R_j$, $S = j \in \{k, ..., l\}$.

After identifying the Join Core tables, tuples that do not find a match in the other operand relation need to be padded with null values for those attributes of the other relation.

Example 7. (Outer-Join). Let us consider Figure. 1 and 2.

$R_1 ⟗ R_2$: $S = 1 \in \{k, ..., l\} \vee 2 \in \{k, ..., l\}$. Only J_1, $J_{1,2,6}$, $J_{2,4,8}$, and $J_{1,2,3,4,5,6,7,8,9}$ satisfy S. The answer is $\{(C, -), (B, b), (-, c) (A, a)\}$. Note that tuples in J_1 and J_8 need to be padded with null values for the set of attributes of the other operand relations, while unwanted components 3, 4, and 5 need to be removed from $J_{1,2,3,4,5,6,7,8,9}$.

$R_1 ⟕ R_2$: $S = 1 \in \{k, ..., l\}$. Only J_1, $J_{1,2,6}$, $J_{1,2,3,4,5,6,7,8,9}$ satisfy S, and the result is $\{(C, -), (B, b), (A, a)\}$.

$R_1 ⟖ R_2$: $S = 2 \in \{k, ..., l\}$. Only $J_{1,2,6}$, $J_{2,4,8}$, $J_{1,2,3,4,5,6,7,8,9}$ satisfy S, and the result is $\{(B, b), (-, c) (A, a)\}$.

4) Anti-Join. An anti-join $R_i \rhd R_j$, defined as $R_i - (R_i \ltimes R_j)$, returns tuples in R_i that do not find a match in R_j. When the outer-join for the edge p was performed during the construction of the Join Core, such tuples (from R_i) must have found no match in R_j and were stored in tables whose names contain i, but not p. Therefore, to answer the query $R_i \rhd R_j$, we look for $J_{k,...,l}$, $i \in \{k, ..., l\} \wedge \neg (p \in \{k, ..., l\})$, namely, $S = i \in \{k, ..., l\} \wedge \neg (p \in \{k, ..., l\})$. Trivial predicate i cannot be omitted.

Example 8. (Anti-Join).

$R_1 \rhd R_2$: $S = 1 \in \{k, ..., l\} \wedge \neg (6 \in \{k, ..., l\})$. Only J_1 satisfies and the answer is $\{C\}$.

$R_2 \rhd R_4$: $S = 2 \in \{k, ..., l\} \wedge \neg (8 \in \{k, ..., l\})$. Only $J_{1,2,6}$ satisfies and the answer is $\{b\}$.

B. Multi-Join Queries

A Join Core consists of regular and extended Join Core tables. For simplicity, we shall not mention explicitly what types of Join Core tables the query predicates are applied to. Readers are advised that if the query is of Type (i), then the selection criteria should be applied to both types of Join Core tables; otherwise, they should only be applied to regular Join Core tables.

Let $E = E_1\ op\ E_2$, where E, E_1, and E_2 are expressions that contain arbitrary legitimate sequences of equi-, semi, outer- and anti-join operators, and op is one of these join operators with a join predicate p. We assume the query graphs for E, E_1, and E_2 are all connected subgraphs of G. Let S_1 and S_2 be the selection criteria on the Join Core tables for E_1 and E_2, respectively, and S the criteria for E. We discuss how to derive S from S_1 and S_2.

1) Equi-Join. Consider $E = E_1 \bowtie E_2$. Each tuple in E is a concatenation of a pair of extended matches in E_1 and E_2 that satisfy p, and such "longer" extended matches must have been captured by successive outer-joins (and complementary joins for cycle-completing relations) performed during the Join Core construction and stored in Join Core tables whose names satisfy $S_1 \wedge S_2 \wedge p \in \{k, ..., l\}$. On the other hand, the components of each tuple in such Join Core tables that satisfy S_1 and S_2 must be result tuples of E_1 and E_2, respectively. In addition, the two components satisfy the join predicate p and thus can generate a result tuple in E. Thus, $S = S_1 \wedge S_2 \wedge p \in \{k, ..., l\}$.

2) Semi-Join. $E = E_1 \ltimes E_2$ and $E = E_1 \rtimes E_2$. As explained, a semi-join is basically an equi-join, except that only the attribute values of one of the operands is retained. Thus, $S = S_1 \wedge S_2 \wedge p \in \{k, ..., l\}$.

3) Outer-Join. $E = E_1 ⟗ E_2$. Tuples in E represent extended matches that come from non-matching tuples of E_1 and E_2, and matching pairs of E_1 and E_2. All these extended match tuples in E were captured by successive outer-joins (and complementary joins for cycle-completing relations) performed during construction of the Join Core and stored in tables whose names satisfy $(S_1 \wedge (\neg p \in \{k, ..., l\})) \vee (S_2 \wedge (\neg p \in \{k, ..., l\})) \vee (S_1 \wedge S_2 \wedge p \in \{k, ..., l\})$, which can be simplified to $S_1 \vee S_2$ because $p \in \{k, ..., l\}$ implies $S_1 \wedge S_2$. On the other hand, each tuple in a Join Core table whose name satisfies $S_1 \vee S_2$ must provide a result tuple to E_1, E_2, or E. Thus, $S = S_1 \vee S_2$. Similarly, for $E_1 ⟕ E_2$, $S = S_1$; for $E_1 ⟖ E_2$, $S = S_2$.

4) Anti-Join. $E = E_1 \rhd E_2$. Tuples in E are extended matches in E_1 that do not find matches in E_2. Thus, tuples in E must have been captured by successive outer-joins (and complementary joins) performed and stored in Join Core tables whose names satisfy S_1 but not ($S_2 \wedge p \in \{k, \ldots, l\}$). On the other hand, Join Core tables whose names satisfy S_1 but not ($S_2 \wedge p \in \{k, \ldots, l\}$) contain tuples of E_1 that do not join with tuples in E_2, which are exactly the result tuples of E. That is, $S = S_1 \wedge \neg(S_2 \wedge p \in \{k, \ldots, l\})$.

Example 9. (Multi-Anti-Join Queries).

$(R_1 \bowtie R_2) \rhd R_3$: $S = 6 \in \{k, \ldots, l\} \wedge \neg (7 \in \{k, \ldots, l\})$. Only $J_{1,2,6}$ satisfies S and the answer is $\{(B, b)\}$.

$(R_2 \rhd R_1) \rhd (R_4 \bowtie R_5)$: $S = (2 \in \{k, \ldots, l\} \wedge \neg (6 \in \{k, \ldots, l\})) \wedge \neg (9 \in \{k, \ldots, l\} \wedge 8 \in \{k, \ldots, l\})$. Only $J_{2,4,8}$ satisfies S, and the answer is $\{(c)\}$.

Theorem 3. Let $E = E_1$ *op* E_2, where E, E_1, and E_2 are arbitrary legitimate expressions that contain equi-, semi-, outer- and anti-joins, and *op* is one of these join operations with a join predicate p. Let S_1 and S_2 be the selection criteria for identifying Join Core tables from which the resulting tuples of E_1 and E_2 can be derived, respectively. Then, the selection criteria S for E is (*i*) if $op = \bowtie$, $S = S_1 \wedge S_2 \wedge p \in \{k, \ldots, l\}$; (*ii*) if $op = \ltimes$ or $\rtimes$, $S = S_1 \wedge S_2 \wedge p \in \{k, \ldots, l\}$; (*iii*) if op = ⟗, $S = S_1 \vee S_2$; if op = ⟖; $S = S_1$; if op = ⟕, $S = S_2$; (*iv*) if $op = \rhd$, $S = S_1 \wedge \neg(S_2 \wedge p \in \{k, \ldots, l\})$.

C. Join Queries with Intersections, Unions, and Differences

Here, we consider join queries with commonly encountered set operators, intersections, unions, and differences. Note that an intersection can be treated as an equi-join in which the join attribute is the primary key. Here, we assume that the join graph includes edges specifying the equalities of primary keys between two schema compatible relations.

Let p be a join predicate specifying the equality of primary key attributes of two schema compatible relations. The intersection operation requires matches in the key values. Consequently, the resulting tuples of $R_i \cap R_j$ can only be found in Join Core tables $J_{k, \ldots, l}$ whose names contain predicate p, i.e., $S = p \in \{k, \ldots, l\}$. This is exactly the same selection criterion as that for an equi-join or a (left or right) semi-join. As for the union operation, the resulting tuples of $R_i \cup R_j$ can be found in Join Core tables whose names contain trivial predicate i or j, i.e., $S = i \in \{k, \ldots, l\} \vee j \in \{k, \ldots, l\}$, the same selection criteria as for a full outer-join. Similarly, for the difference operation, the resulting tuples of $R_i - R_j$ can be found in Join Core tables whose indices contain the trivial predicate i, but not j, i.e., $S = i \in \{k, \ldots, l\} \wedge \neg (j \in \{k, \ldots, l\})$, the same selection criteria as for an anti-join.

By the same reasoning as presented in the previous section (*B*) and Theorem 3, we can extend the usage of Join Core tables to queries with arbitrary legitimate sequences of unions, differences, and intersections, in addition to equi-, semi-, outer- and anti-joins. The theorem follows.

Theorem 4. Let $E = E_1$ *op* E_2, where E, E_1, and E_2 are arbitrary legitimate expressions that contain equi-joins, semi-joins, outer-joins, anti-joins, unions, differences, and intersections, and *op* is one of these operations with a join predicate p. Let S_1 and S_2 be the selection criteria for identifying Join Core tables from which the result tuples of E_1 and E_2 can be derived, respectively. Then, the selection criteria S for E is (*i*) if $op = \bowtie$ or $\cap$, $S = S_1 \wedge S_2 \wedge p \in \{k, \ldots, l\}$; (*ii*) if $op = \ltimes$ or $\rtimes$, $S = S_1 \wedge S_2 \wedge p \in \{k, \ldots, l\}$; (*iii*) if op = ⟗ or $\cup$, $S = S_1 \vee S_2$; if op = ⟖, $S = S_1$; if op = ⟕, $S = S_2$; (*iv*) if $op = \rhd$ or $-$, $S = S_1 \wedge \neg(S_2 \wedge p \in \{k, \ldots, l\})$.

VII. COST ANALYSIS

In this section, we analyze the time and space consumption of using Join Core. In addition, we also discuss measures to reduce the size of Join Core.

A) Time Consumptions

1) Disk Accesses Time

To answer a query, Join Core tables containing the result tuples are read into memory. Thus, the total number of disk accesses is dependent upon the size of the query result, not the complexity of the query.

2) CPU Time

Once desired Join Core tables are read into memory, all that is remaining is to perform equality checking between alias components (of cycle-completing relations), pad "missing" attributes with null values (for outer-join operations), and eliminate unwanted attributes and duplicates. All these tasks should take only a very small amount of CPU time.

B) Space Consumptions

To simplify discussions, we assume no dangling tuple exists in any of the equi-joins in the graph, which represents a worst case space consumption scenario since dangling tuples can shorten the matches. We further assume that in each join, all tuples of a relation find exactly the same number of matches in the other relation, namely a uniformity assumption on the matching of a join.

Consider a join between R_i (with T_i tuples), and R_j (with T_j tuples). We shall call T_j/T_i, denoted as r_{ij}, *the join ratio* of T_i with respect to T_j, that is, the average number of matches found in R_j for each tuple in R_i. In a one-many relationship from R_i to R_j, $r_{ij} \geq 1$. On the other hand, in a many-one relationship from R_i to R_j, $T_j/T_i \leq 1$. Since each tuple in R_i still can find one match in R_j, as we have assumed no dangling tuples exist in the joins, r_{ij} is set to 1 (i.e., $r_{ij}=1$) when $T_j/T_i \leq 1$.

To estimate the size of a Join Core, we first estimate the total number of match tuples, denoted by M, in the Join Core, and multiply it by the length of each match tuple.

To estimate the number of different matches, we can start from any relation, say R_i, by setting $M = T_i$, and then marking R_i as visited. For each edge $\langle R_i, R_j \rangle$, where R_i is a visited node while R_j is not, $M=M \times r_{ij}$. Once all relations are visited, the final M is the estimate.

Now, let us compute the length of each match tuple. Let e be the number of join edges and n the number of relations in the join graph. Each outer-join adds the set of attributes of one relation to the schema of the output, recalling the construction of a Join Core. Therefore, the final output of the outer-joins consists of the values of the attributes of $e+1$ relations, $e+1 \geq n$. For simplicity of analysis, we assume tuples in all relations have the same or a similar length L. Therefore, the size the Join Core is

$$M \times (e+1) \times L \tag{1}$$

As compared to the database size $T_{avg} \times n \times L$, where $T_{avg}=Avg\{T_1, \ldots, T_n\}$ is the average number of tuples in a relation.

Note that when all relations are of similar sizes, i.e., $T_{avg} \approx T_1 \approx \ldots \approx T_n$, all r_{ij}'s ≈ 1 and $M \approx T_{avg}$. In addition, if the graph has no (or few) cycles, i.e., $e+1=(\approx)\ n$, the Join Core size would be close to the database size, that is, $M \times (e+1) \times L \approx T_{avg} \times n \times L$, which is the best case scenario.

C) Space Reduction Methods

Many data compression techniques [4][5][13] can be used to compress the Join Core. Here, we shall only discuss methods that are specifically related to the reduction of the Join Core structure.

Storing all join relationships of a complex graph can consume large amounts of space. Here, we discuss heuristics that can significantly reduce the space consumption of the Join Cores, however, at the price of incurring additional join operations. Further research is still needed to analyze the cost and benefits of these heuristics.

(H1). Store only useful relations, relationships, and attribute values. Statistics and knowledge on the usages of relations, relationships, and attributes may be available or can be collected to assist in making such decisions.

(H2). Remove smaller relations from a join graph. Smaller relations, in terms of the numbers of tuples in the relations, need replicate their tuples more times to generate M match tuples, which will make updates (on smaller relations) more expensive. In addition, if a removed relation is referenced in a join query, then a join operation must be performed. Removing smaller relations incurs less penalty because joins with smaller relations are faster to perform. Moreover, smaller relations have better chances of fitting in memory to make the joins faster.

(H3). Remove cycle-completing relations. Removal of a cycle-completing relation from a graph implies removal of all its aliases too, which can significantly reduce the storage consumption. Since any graph traversal method can be used in construction a Join Core, one is given the opportunity to select "good" relations to be cycle-completing relations. Here, we recommend relations that are small (following H2) and, if possible, complete multiple cycles.

1) Constructing Join Core with Space Constraint

Without detailed cost-benefit measures, here is a simple way to construct a Join Core that satisfies a given space limit. First, one can, following (H1), remove unwanted relations, relationships, and attributes if a priori knowledge or statistics are available. If the Join Core is still too large, one can consider removing a smallest relation, following (H2), or a cycle-completing relation, following (H3), until the desirable size is met.

VI. NEO4J GRAPH DATABASE

In this section, we discuss Neo4j in details as it will be used in later performance evaluation against Join Core.

Neo4j is most popular graph databases according to [24]. It is an open-source graph database management system that provides high scalability and read/write performance [24]. The high performance is mainly owing to the use of both a native processing and storage model. Native processing model is referred to the leverage of index-free adjacency (where related nodes are physically connected to each other) in graph database. The use of index- free means that the query time depends on the searched graph length rather than the total size of the graph [4]. On the other hand, native storage model refers to the underlying physical structure of the database, where nodes and relationships are stored in a graph structure. This technology ensures that the graph database is optimized by storing related entities close to each other [24].

Neo4j employs the property graph data model [24]. Property graph model consists of nodes, relationship, properties and labels [7]. Both node and relationship hold a number of properties that are stored in the form of key-value pairs. Relationship links nodes to each other and each relationship has a name, direction and start and end nodes. Labels tag nodes to group them, and to identify their role in the dataset. Figure. 5 explains the consumer complaints against the company's products and sub-products, and issues that rose and the company's responses to. Each and every node is associated with the labels and the properties.

In Neo4j, each type of element is stored in a separate data store. For instance, physical file neostore.nodestore.db contains all nodes in the dataset where neostore.propertystore.db and neostore. relationshipstore.db stores properties and relationship, respectively [7]. Records inside node and relationship data store are fixed in size which accelerates record lookups in the file, as any known record ID can be used compute the record's location in the file.

Neo4j can be queried in many ways, such as Traverser API and Cypher query language [17]. Cypher is a declarative graph query language provides an efficient way to create, update and query the graph database [3]. It is considered as a

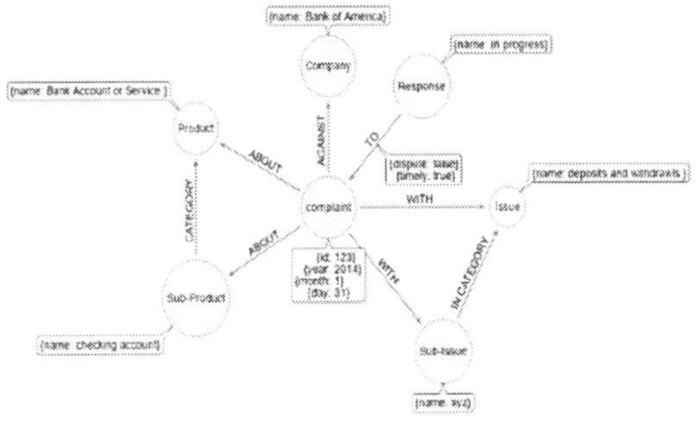

Figure 5. The labelled property graph Model

powerful language that focuses on what to get rather than how to get it. Cypher's structure is inspired by SQL to make it easier and more familiar for the SQL users, although it focuses on finding and describing patterns in the graph.

Cypher uses clauses (like most query languages) to query from the graph, a simple read query would be consist of MATCH, WHERE and RETURN clauses. Cypher execution engine optimizes and turn each query into an execution plan. The plan is a pattern of number of connected operators, where each operator is responsible for a small section of the query execution.

VII. EXPERIMENTAL RESULTS

A) Space Consumptions

We have performed experiments on the graph database NEO4J 3.0.6 community edition along with the Join Core to compare their performance efficiency. We have performed all experiments on a laptop computer with a 2.40 GHz CPU, 8GB RAM, and a 1 TB hard drive. 1.2GB consumer complaint dataset was generated. Consumer Complaints dataset has 4 relations, i.e. Product table, Issue table, Response table and Complaint table. The dataset which we took was from the Neo4j dataset. After processing the dataset in the join core tables, we get 3 GB dataset. These tables are stored in the hard disk. The larger size of Join Core is due to replications of tuples of relations. Similarly, after loading all the data and the relationships between them in the Neo4j database we get a data size of 2.4GB. The data is stored in the disks. The increase in the size of the database is due to summation of actual size of database, ratio of size of graph.db to index and ratio of size of graph.db to schema [24]. Table 1 shows the size of Join Core and Neo4j.

TABLE 1. SPACE CONSUMPTIONS

Consumer Complaint Dataset	**Join Core**	**Neo4j**
1.2 GB	3 GB	2.4 GB

B) Query Processing Time

We measure the elapsed time of the test queries. In Neo4j, the consumer complaint dataset has some cypher queries in [23]. We use the same queries and modify them to be worked in Join Core. While keeping (most of) the selections and projections, we remove any "group by", "order by", "limit", aggregate functions, from the queries so that we can focus mainly on the join query processing. We add "distinct" to the queries as we have implicitly assumed the set semantics in the paper.

Join Core tables are read from disks into memory for processing, and the result tuples are written back to the disks. Elapsed time measures the time from beginning to end, after writing all result tuples to the disks.

Table 2 shows the query processing time. In the first column, the ID of the consumer complaint query is shown first, followed by the relations involved in the join operations. For simplicity, relations are referenced by the numbers assigned to them in Figure. 6. All times are measured in milliseconds.

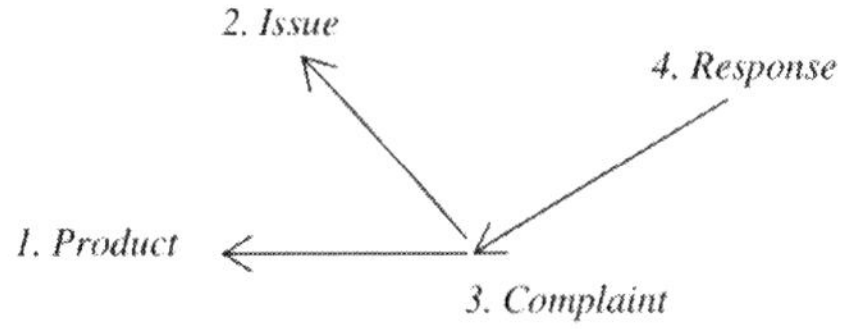

Figure 6. Consumer Complaints Join Graph

With Join Cores, all queries saw their first responses instantly. As explained, all it takes is the retrieval of a block of a relevant Join Core table into memory and simple manipulations before output it after simple manipulations.

The result size of the query, not the complexity determines the query processing time because the join result is readily available in the Join Core. Queries 2 and 3 best illustrate this characteristic of Join core. Query 2 has only one join but generates large numbers of result tuples. On the other hand, Query 3 has two joins, but generates much smaller numbers of result tuples. Therefore, it took much longer to process Query 2 than Query 3. As shown in Table 2, in Join Core, it took 253milliseconds to process Query 2 for 1.2 GB dataset, but it took only 13milliseconds, respectively, to process Query 3. Since there were no joins to perform in the Join Core, many queries completed instantly. Whereas in Neo4j, path traversal operations in the complex relationships of nodes determines the query processing time because in Neo4j, it first travels through the relationship table and then retrieves the resultant tuples from the disk. Queries 1 and 6 are best to illustrate this characteristic of Neo4j. Both queries 1 and 6 have no joins. But the complexities of relationships involved in the query makes to retrieve small number of result tuples in more time compared to query 1, which retrieved large number of result tuples in less time compared to query 6.

From the results, it can be inferred that, if the query has the complex relationships in it then Neo4j takes more time than the join core. From the above experimental results, it can be observed that when the queries require large joins one can use join core, which is portable and can be used for any application domain irrespective of the API. Join Core retrieve results instantly when compared to the Neo4j. From this study, it can be concluded that to process complex queries join core is the best option irrespective of the size of the data.

Another advantage of the proposed methodology is that it does not consume much memory. All it needs is to build a hash table for the final duplicate elimination.

We believe the instant responses, fast query processing, and small memory consumption of the Join Core are well worth its required additional storage space.

TABLE 2. TIME CONSUMPTIONS

Query		Join Core	Neo4j	Result
		Elapsed Time (ms)	Elapsed Time (ms)	Tuples
1	R_2	18	714	68
2	$\bowtie \{R_1, R_4\}$	253	31,824	1,976
3	$\bowtie \{R_1, R_2, R_3\}$	13	262	18
4	$\bowtie \{R_1, R_2, R_4\}$	49	317	447
5	R_2	19	319	95
6	R_3	18	130	5
7	R_4	17	860	7
8	$\bowtie \{R_2, R_3, R_4\}$	19	752	84
9	$\bowtie \{R_2, R_4\}$	19	856	106

VIII. CONCLUSIONS AND FUTURE WORK

In this paper, an anti-relational approach, called Join Core, has been presented. Join Core technique stores the equi-join relationships of tuples on various tables. The join queries can be answered quickly by merely merging these tables without having to perform expensive joins. We use Neo4j as graph database to perform experiments and compare its time and space consumptions with a Join Core. Preliminary experimental results showed that Join Core outperforms Neo4j when complex join queries are processed. This is because in Join Core, there was no need to perform join operations at run time while in Neo4j, the path traversal operations depend upon the complexities of the relationships of tuples. In the future work, we will implement all possible scenarios discussed in the above sections, such as the semi-join, outer- or anti-join. We will also perform experiments in the SSD and compare the performance with the hard disk. Furthermore, we will assess the impact of the page cache size used in Neo4j.

REFERENCES

[1] A. Levy, A. Mendelzon, Y. Sagiv, and D. Srivastava, "Answering queries using views", In ACM PODS Conf., 1995, pp. 95-104.

[2] B. He, K. Yang, R. Fang, M. Lu, N. Govindaraju, Q. Luo, and P. Sander, "Relational joins on graphics processors", In ACM SIGMOD Conf., 2008, pp. 511-524.

[3] B. Kenny, Understanding How Neo4j Cypher Queries are Evaluated: http://www.kennybastani.com/2014/07/understanding-how-neo4j-cypher-queries.html, [retrieved: 12, 2017].

[4] C. Kim, E. Sedlar, and J. Chhugani, "Sort vs. Hash Revisited: Fast Join Implementation on Modern Multi-Core CPUs", In VLDB Conf., 2009, pp. 1378-1389.

[5] D. Abadi, S. Madden, and M. Ferreira, "Integrating Compression and Execution in Column-Oriented Database Systems", In SIGMOD, 2006, pp. 671–682.

[6] D. DeWitt and R. Gerber, "Multiprocessor hash-based join algorithms", In VLDB, 1985, pp. 151–164.

[7] E. Eifrem, J. Webber and I. Robinson, Graph Databases. 2nd Edition "O'Reilly Media, Inc.", 2015

[8] H. Karloff and M. Mihail, "On the complexity of the view-selection problem", In ACM PODS Conf., 1999, pp. 167-173.

[9] J. Goldstein and P.-A. Larson, "Optimizing queries using materialized views: a practical, scalable solution", In ACM SIGMOD, 2001, pp. 331-342.

[10] J. Yang, K. Karlapalem, and Q. Li, "Algorithms for materialized view design in data warehousing environment", In VLDB, 1997, pp. 25-29.

[11] M. Kitsuregawa, H. Tanaka, and T. Moto-Oka, "Application of hash to data base machine and its architecture", New Generation Computing 1(1), 1983, pp. 63-74.

[12] M. W. Blasgen and K. P. Eswaran, "Storage and access in relational data bases", IBM Systems Journal 16.4, 1977, pp. 363-377.

[13] M. Zukowski, S. Héman, N. Nes, and P. Boncz, "Super-scalar RAM-CPU cache compression", In ICDE, 2006, - http://doi.org/10.1109/ICDE.2006.150.

[14] P. Valduriez, "Join indices", ACM Transactions on Database Systems (TODS), 1987, 12(2), pp. 218-246.

[15] R. Derakhshan, F. Dehne, O. Korn, and B. Stantic, "Simulated Annealing for Materialized View Selection in Data Warehousing Environment", In Databases and applications, 2006, pp. 89-94.

[16] R. Pottinger and A. Levy, "A scalable algorithm for answering queries using views", In VLDB Conf., 2000, pp. 484-495.

[17] R. Kaliyar, Graph Databases: A Survey, International Conference on Computing, Communication and Automation (ICCCA2015), p785-790

[18] R. De Virgilio, A. Maccioni, and R. Torlone, Converting Relational to Graph Databases. In First International Workshop on Graph Data Management Experiences and Systems (GRADES '13), 2013, pp. 1–6, New York, New York, USA, ACM Press.

[19] S. Agarawal, S. Chaudhuri, and V. Narasayya, "Automated Selection of Materialized Views and Indexes for SQL Databases", In VLDB , 2000, pp. 496-505.

[20] S. Chu, M. Balazinska, and D. Suciu, "From Theory to Practice: Efficient Join Query Evaluation in a Parallel Database System", In ACM SIGMOD Conf., 2015, pp. 63-78.

[21] Z. Li, and K. A. Ross, "Fast joins using join indices", The VLDB Journal—The International Journal on Very Large Data Bases", 1999, 8(1), pp. 1-24.

[22] M. Hamdi, F. Yu, S. Alswedani, and W.C. Hou, "Storing Join Relationships for Fast Join Query Processing". In International Conference on Database and Expert Systems Applications (DEXA), 2017, pp. 167-177. Springer, Cham..

[23] Importing CSV Data into Neo4j, https://neo4j.com/developer/guide-import-csv/#load-csv-webinar , [retrieved: 1, 2018].

[24] Graph database (Neo4J): https://neo4j.com, , [retrieved: 1, 2018].

Graph Learning for Prediction of Drug-Disease Interactions: Preliminary Results

Andrej Kastrin* and Dimitar Hristovski†
Institute of Biostatistics and Medical Informatics, Faculty of Medicine, University of Ljubljana
Ljubljana, Slovenia
Email: *andrej.kastrin@mf.uni-lj.si, †dimitar.hristovski@mf.uni-lj.si

Abstract—**One of the fundamental problems to complex network research is understanding of link formation. We study the problem of representation learning in a bipartite drug-disease network of semantic predications extracted from biomedical literature. We employ DeepWalk and node2vec node embedding methods with deep learning link predictor, as well as standard baseline predictors including common neighbors, Jaccard coefficient, and Adamic/Adar. Experimental results show that both network embedding algorithms outperform traditional link predictors.**

Keywords–Complex networks; Network analysis; Network learning; MEDLINE.

I. Introduction

The corpus of biomedical papers is growing at an exponential rate. For instance, MEDLINE [1], the largest bibliographic database in biomedicine, at the time of this writing, aggregates more than 28 million citations to life science papers. However, a significant amount of potentially useful knowledge still remains undiscovered. It is hard to synthesize divergent research evidence into coherently interpretable knowledge. Here, we tackle the problem of unravelling hidden relations between drugs and diseases using link prediction methodology from biomedical literature.

An elementary problem in graph research is the analysis of the connections between the nodes. In computer science and statistics, this is known as link prediction problem. Although novel research area, link prediction attracted numerous researchers in the last decade. Link prediction refers to the discovery of relations between nodes that are not connected in the current snapshot of a given network but will be connected in the future. The aim of link prediction in general is to estimate the probability that a link exists among a pair of nodes, based on the topology of existing nodes, edges, and their attributes.

In the case of link prediction, we need to encode pairwise properties between nodes, such as the number of common neighbors or relationship strength. Traditional approaches rely on summary network statistics (e.g., centrality measures) to extract structural information from networks. However, recently, approaches have emerged that seek to learn representations that encode structural information about the network and present a powerful alternative to traditional feature engineering. The general idea behind representation learning is to learn a mapping that embeds nodes as points in a low-dimensional vector space (i.e., embedding space). The goal is to optimize this mapping so that geometric relationships in this space reflect the structure of the original network. The learned embeddings can then be used as feature inputs for machine learning tasks. Embedding methods can be generally categorized into three groups [2]: (i) factorization methods (e.g., locally linear embedding [3]), (ii) random walk techniques (e.g., DeepWalk [4], node2vec [5]), and (iii) deep learning (e.g., structural deep network embedding [6]).

In this work, we investigate the performance of two network embedding algorithms, namely DeepWalk and node2vec. More formally, we examine, how neural network predictor, using computed embeddings from DeepWalk and node2vec, behaves on the task of link prediction in a large-scale network of semantic predications extracted from biomedical literature. In addition, we examine these methods in contrast to traditional baseline predictors such as common neighbors, Jaccard coefficient, and Adamic/Adar.

The rest of the paper is structured as follows. In Section II, we present dataset and methodology used in this study. Results are presented in Section III. Finally, we conclude in Section IV.

II. Methods

A. Dataset

SemRep is a symbolic natural language processing tool that extracts semantic predications from MEDLINE citations [7]. A predication is a formal representation of textual content that consists of a subject, predicate, and object. Subject and object arguments are concepts from the Unified Medical Language System (UMLS) Metathesaurus [8] as available through MetaMap [9]. The predicate is from UMLS Semantic Network [10]. These predications provide a normalized representation of the meaning of the source text in a machine-readable form for automatic processing. SemRep extracts about 30 predicate types, related to clinical medicine (e.g., `TREATS`, `DIAGNOSES`), substance interactions (e.g., `INTERACTS_WITH`, `STIMULATES`), genetic etiology of disease (e.g., `ASSOCIATED_WITH`), and pharmacogenomics (e.g., `AFFECTS`). In this paper, we focus only on `TREATS` relation. We extract all `TREATS` relations that connect drugs (Metathesaurus concepts with semantic type "Pharmacologic Substance") and diseases (concepts with semantic type "Disease or Syndrome").

B. Baseline Predictors

We implemented a link prediction baseline using various proximity measures, which are used to find similarity among a pair of nodes. Our assumption is that similar nodes are more likely to form a link in the future. For each non-observed link (u, v) in a testing network, a link prediction computes a score $s(u, v)$, which can be considered as an estimate of the presence of edge creation between nodes u and v. In our initial settings we used common neighbors, Jaccard coefficient, and Adamic/Adar.

C. Network Embeddings

For network representation learning models, we used two state-of-the-art algorithms, namely DeepWalk [4] and node2vec [5]. Both methods employ random walk algorithm to sample topological properties and node representations are learned to preserve pairwise similarities of nodes.

DeepWalk learns an embedding by sampling random walks from each node and applying skip-gram learning on those walks. We use the default parameters described in the seminal paper, i.e., walk length $t = 80$, number of walks per node $\gamma = 80$, and window size $w = 10$. node2vec improves the random walk step of DeepWalk by defining hyperparameters p and q that control the depth and breadth of random walks, respectively. The special case with parameters $p = 1$ and $q = 1$ corresponds to DeepWalk. In our settings we used the same values for parameters as for DeepWalk; the remaining parameters were set to $p = 2$ and $q = 4$.

After network embedding, we need to set up a statistical classification framework for link prediction. Both algorithms, DeepWalk and node2vec, described above, are designed to learn feature representations for nodes in a network. However, in our study we are interested in prediction involving pairs of nodes and not individual nodes. To this end, we need to define a binary operator $\circ$ over the corresponding feature vectors $f(u)$ and $f(v)$ in order to generate a composite representation $g(u, v)$. We consider three different alternatives for the $\circ$ operator:

1) concatenation: $u_i + v_i$,
2) average: $(u_i + v_i)/2$, and
3) Hadamard product: $(u_i * v_i)$,

where u and v are two vectors and u_i and v_i are i-th element of u and v, respectively.

D. Machine Learning

For the classification task, we use deep learning model implemented in TensorFlow [11] as feed-forward neural network with a single hidden layer. Input to the model is a vector representation with the binary operator defined above. The output of the model is a probability of a link formation between the input nodes. We draw a fixed proportion of the existing edges for training, and use the rest of edges for the testing. Training was defined for a time period from 1843 to 2003 and testing for a time range from 2004 to 2018.

In this study, we used the following five measures to compare the performance of the statistical learning: area under a receiver operating characteristic curve (AUROC), area under a precision-recall curve (AUPR), mean average precision (mAP), and precision at k (Prec@k).

III. Results and Discussion

In our experiment we used the knowledge network, constructed as a subset of SemMedDB network [12], as defined previously in the Methods section. The network comprises 13,182 unique vertices that refer to drugs and 8856 vertices that refer to diseases. In total, there were 170,707 relations between both sets of nodes. The mean degree of the bipartite network was 12.95 links and the average path length was 1.76 hops.

The results in terms of classification performances of the performed experiment are summarized in Table I. The best performer across all four performance measures is node2vec with average merge type. If we consider only AUROC and AUPR measures, the baseline predictors are slightly better than DeepWalk and node2vec. Common neighbors measure performs best, followed by Jaccard coefficient, and Adamic/Adar. mAP and Prec@k scores for DeepWalk and node2vec are an order of magnitude higher in comparison to baseline predictors.

TABLE I. Performance Measures of Link Prediction Algorithms

Method	Binary operator	AUROC	AUPR	Pred@k	mAP
CN	–	0.86	0.86	0.86	0.64
JC	–	0.85	0.84	0.86	0.62
AA	–	0.81	0.74	0.82	0.54
	Co	0.83	0.86	0.96	0.79
DeepWalk	Av	0.83	0.86	0.97	0.80
	Ha	0.72	0.72	0.82	0.65
	Co	0.83	0.86	0.96	0.80
node2vec	Av	0.83	0.86	0.97	0.81
	Ha	0.72	0.73	0.83	0.65

Note: CN = Common Neighbors, JC = Jaccard Coefficient, AA = Adamic/Adar; (Co)ncatenate, (Av)erage, and (Ha)damard merge type; further details are provided in text

As far as we know, this is the first work discussing knowledge network, network embeddings as well as deep learning approach to discover new drug-disease interactions from literature. Results of this study show that both network embedding algorithms, DeepWalk and node2vec, outperform traditional link predictors such as common neighbors or Jaccard coefficient.

IV. Conclusion

We investigate the representation learning in bipartite drug-disease network of semantic predications. We design a deep learning model that includes the network structure into the embedding. Experimental results demonstrated that performance measures in terms of AUROC and AUPR are comparable. However, we found evidence that DeepWalk and node2vec outperformed baseline predictors in terms of Pred@k and mAP measures.

References

[1] "PubMed," https://www.ncbi.nlm.nih.gov/pubmed, accessed: 2019-06-27.

[2] P. Goyal and E. Ferrara, "Graph embedding techniques, applications, and performance: A survey," Knowledge-Based Systems, vol. 151, 2018, pp. 78–94.

[3] S. T. Roweis and L. K. Saul, "Nonlinear dimensionality reduction by locally linear embedding," Science, vol. 290, no. 5500, 2000, pp. 2323–2326.

[4] B. Perozzi, R. Al-Rfou, and S. Skiena, "Deepwalk: Online learning of social representations," in Proceedings of the 20th ACM SIGKDD International Conference on Knowledge Discovery and Data Mining. ACM, 2014, pp. 701–710.

[5] A. Grover and J. Leskovec, "node2vec: Scalable feature learning for networks," in Proceedings of the 22nd ACM SIGKDD International Conference on Knowledge Discovery and Data Mining. ACM, 2016, pp. 855–864.

[6] D. Wang, P. Cui, and W. Zhu, "Structural deep network embedding," in Proceedings of the 22nd ACM SIGKDD international conference on Knowledge discovery and data mining. ACM, 2016, pp. 1225–1234.

[7] T. C. Rindflesch and M. Fiszman, "The interaction of domain knowledge and linguistic structure in natural language processing: Interpreting hypernymic propositions in biomedical text," Journal of Biomedical Informatics, vol. 36, no. 6, 2003, pp. 462–477.

[8] O. Bodenreider, "The Unified Medical Language System (UMLS): Integrating biomedical terminology," Nucleic Acids Research, vol. 32, no. Database issue, 2004, pp. D267–D270.

[9] A. R. Aronson and F.-M. Lang, "An overview of MetaMap: Historical perspective and recent advances," Journal of the American Medical Informatics Association, vol. 17, no. 3, 2010, pp. 229–236.

[10] D. A. Lindberg, B. L. Humphreys, and A. T. McCray, "The Unified Medical Language System," Methods of Information in Medicine, vol. 32, Aug. 1993, pp. 281–291.

[11] M. Abadi, P. Barham, J. Chen, Z. Chen, A. Davis, J. Dean, M. Devin, S. Ghemawat, G. Irving, M. Isard et al., "Tensorflow: A system for large-scale machine learning," in 12th USENIX Symposium on Operating Systems Design and Implementation (OSDI '16), 2016, pp. 265–283.

[12] H. Kilicoglu, D. Shin, M. Fiszman, G. Rosemblat, and T. C. Rindflesch, "SemMedDB: A PubMed-scale repository of biomedical semantic predications," Bioinformatics, vol. 28, no. 23, 2012, pp. 3158–3160.

Exploring and Comparing Table Fragments With Fragment Summaries

Fatma-Zohra Hannou
Sorbonne Université, CNRS, LIP6
4, place Jussieu
75252 Paris, France
Email: Fatma.Hannou@lip6.fr

Bernd Amann
Sorbonne Université, CNRS, LIP6
4, place Jussieu
75252 Paris, France
Email: Bernd.Amann@lip6.fr

Mohamed-Amine Baazizi
Sorbonne Université, CNRS, LIP6
4, place Jussieu
75252 Paris, France
Email: Mohamed-Amine.Baazizi@lip6.fr

***Abstract*—In this article, we introduce a new pattern-based summarization framework for representing and *reasoning* about fragmented data sets. A *fragment summary* is a concise, complete and precise representation of a data fragment and its information contents *relatively to the whole data set*. We formally define the notion of fragment summary and the use of Structured Query Language (SQL) queries over fragment summaries for analyzing data fragments. We introduce an algorithm for computing summaries and present an experimental evaluation using two real-life data sets.**

***Keywords*–data fragments; summarization; patterns; reasoning.**

I. Introduction

Summarization is the process of generating a concise representation of a data set for some specific processing tasks. Compared to data compression, the goal of summarization is, usually, to preserve enough information for fulfilling these tasks without the need for decompression. Data summarization has been applied to various data types (text, data streams, graphs, structured data, music, etc.) for different tasks related to information retrieval, data monitoring, data visualization, query processing, and data integration as witnessed by recent works [1]–[5].

In this article, we introduce a new pattern-based summarization framework for representing and *analyzing* fragmented data sets. A *fragment summary* is a concise representation of a data fragment and its information contents *relative to the whole data set*. Data fragments can be the result of user-defined filtering queries or any other data extraction task over some data set. They can also correspond to data tables (sources) that partially cover a complete reference table like a dimension table in some analytic data set. Fragment summaries can then be used to rapidly *decide if a data tuple or a category of tuples (defined by attribute/value pairs) is completely or partially included* in the corresponding data fragment.

To better understand the potential of fragment summaries, consider **Energy** in Table I reporting the daily energy consumption for rooms (ro) in two floors (fl). The table contains a tuple for each location and time defined by the week (we) and the day (da), and indicates missing information with Null. The first data fragment is defined by query Q_{avail} returning all tuples with existing kWh values. The second fragment, denoted with Q_{miss}, contains all tuple identifiers with missing kWh values ; it is complementary to the first fragment. Both fragment summaries are presented in Table II. A fragment summary corresponds to a table of *patterns* that concisely

TABLE I. DATA TABLE

Energy	fl	ro	we	da	kWh
t_0	f1	r1	w1	Mon	10
t_1	f1	r1	w1	Tue	12
t_2	f1	r1	w2	Mon	10
m_0	f1	r1	w2	Tue	Null
t_3	f1	r2	w1	Mon	8
t_4	f1	r2	w1	Tue	10
m_1	f1	r2	w2	Mon	Null
m_2	f1	r2	w2	Tue	Null
t_5	f2	r1	w1	Mon	12
t_6	f2	r1	w1	Tue	7
t_7	f2	r1	w2	Mon	8
t_8	f2	r1	w2	Tue	8

TABLE II. FRAGMENT SUMMARIES OF Q_{AVAIL} AND Q_{MISS}

P_{avail}	fl	ro	we	da
p_0	*	*	w1	*
p_1	f2	*	*	*
p_2	f1	r1	*	Mon

P_{miss}	fl	ro	we	da
p_3	*	r2	w2	*
p_4	f1	r1	w2	Tue

summarizes all *data categories* contained in the fragment. The summary P_{avail} describes all complete categories of available information (for example, all values are available for category [we='w1'] and any sub-category), whereas the summary P_{miss} describes all empty categories (*e.g.* all values are missing for category [ro='r2', we='w2']). Observe that both fragment summaries contain the *minimal set of all attribute/value pairs* that are necessary to precisely characterize this fragment (and all categories it subsumes). For example, categories [fl='f1', ro='r1'] and [we='w2'] are not subsumed by any pattern in both tables and therefore contain tuples with missing and with available measures. Observe also that the intersection of both summaries is empty and the union is the "wildcard" template $*$ covering the whole data set.

Fragments summaries are meant to provide a precise semantic characterization of data fragments and, thus, can be exploited for performing complex analytical tasks such as analyzing the *completeness* and *correctness* of analytic aggregation queries. To illustrate this case, consider the following query over the original data table **Energy**(fl, ro, we, da, kWh):

```
select fl, ro, we, sum(kWh) from Energy
  group by fl, ro, we
```

By examining this data table, it is easy to notice that the computed *sum* for the partition [f1,r1,w1] is be *incorrect* since this partition is *incomplete*. This examination allows inferring that no value is returned for the partition [f1,r2,w2] whose values are *missing*. Fragment summaries are very useful in supporting such analysis tasks especially when data becomes large and not amenable to visual inspection ; in this case, SQL turns out to be helpful as illustrated with the following queries over fragment summaries:

- `select fl,ro, we from` P_{avail} `where da='*'` retrieves the summary of all partitions with a correct aggregation result (e.g., the fragment characterized with week=w1 and floor=f2)
- `select fl,ro, we from` P_{avail} `where da<>'*'` returns the partitions with incorrect results (all results are incorrect for room 'r1' at floor 'f1') and
- `select fl,ro, we from` P_{miss} `where da='*'` characterizes the missing results (all results are missing for room 'r2' at week 'w2').

Fragment summaries characterize *all* complete categories in a fragment and their compactness ratio (summary size/fragment size) can be very high (see Section VI). This space loss is compensated by the speedup of complex decision tasks, such as identifying complete and missing data and annotating incorrect query results.

In our previous example, all fragments (and their summaries) were defined over a set of attributes that are part of the table *key*. In this case, the summary of any fragment is "complete" in the sense that it allows to decide for each tuple if it is part of the fragment or not. It is also possible to build summaries over sets of attributes that are insufficient to separate fragment tuples from non-fragment tuples. In this case, some tuple categories can be formally identified as belonging to some fragment, but other categories may be non-distinguishable.

To illustrate the notion of non-distinguishable (ND) fragments, consider the Adult dataset [6] that is widely used for learning population classes based on income. This dataset reports census data about income for $32,561$ individuals described by 14 attributes including one numerical attribute *Age* with domain $[17, 90]$ and seven categorical attributes *Workclass*, *Education*, *Marital-Status*, *Occupation*, *Race*, *Sex* and *Income* [<50k,≥50k]. In [7], this data-set was used for producing approximate summaries of highly frequent data categories. An example of such a summary is the one stating that 69% of individuals with *[race='White', sex='Male', Marital-Status='married-civ-spouse']* have a high-income (i.e., >50K). Instead of producing approximate summaries, we are interested in obtaining exact ones by exploiting additional attributes like: *Age*, *Workclass*, *Education* and *Occupation* and classify the individuals into High, Low and Non-Distinguishable (ND) as reported in Table III.

Here, we can see that (1) all white married male soldiers between 40 and 50 and all employees of the federal government with a PhD have a high income, (2) all white married males that have a low income, are young or have never worked or have a preschool diploma and (3) it is not possible to decide for white married males with a Master degree, or are old with a PhD, whether they belong to high or low-income class. We will show in Section V how this kind of detailed analysis can be done by evaluating simple SQL queries over pre-computed fragment summaries.

TABLE III. "MARRIED-WHITE-MALE" FRAGMENT

High

age	workc	education	occupation
40-50	*	*	Armed-Forces
*	federal-gov	Doctorate	*

Low

age	workc	education	occupation
< 20	*	*	*
*	Never-worked	*	*
*	*	Preschool	*

ND

age	workc	education	occupation
*	*	Masters	*
> 60	*	Doctorate	*

Contributions: In this article, we formalize the notion of fragment summary and show how fragment summaries can be exploited for characterizing data fragments in data sets and query results. Our approach leverages the relational representation of fragment summaries by taking advantage of SQL for achieving these different analyses. We introduce an algorithm for efficiently generating fragment summaries and sketch a mechanism for reasoning on fragment summaries to gain knowledge about data.

Outline: This article is organized as follows. In Section II, we survey related work before introducing our data model in Section III. Sections IV and V are dedicated to presenting the fragment generation algorithm and the reasoning mechanism, respectively. Experimentation results are discussed in Section VI, and we conclude the article in Section VII.

II. Related Work

Our contribution lies in the intersection of two mainstream topics: data summarization and relative data completeness, which is a special case of data completeness. We report on works addressing both topics.

A. Data summarization

The main goal of most approaches in this family is to reduce the data size while preserving as much information as deemed useful for achieving specific operations like evaluating aggregate queries [4] or returning approximate answers with correctness guarantees [1]. Different techniques are used. Some approaches exploit semantic knowledge like fuzzy thesauri and linguistic variables [8][9] or OLAP hierarchies [2][3] to generate concise descriptions of large data sets. Efficient encoding of data has also been used for compressing columns and rows [10] but our work is more reminiscent to the family of *pattern mining* approaches [7][11][12] where summaries are expressed using patterns. In [7], summaries are built by selecting the most representative patterns that capture the largest fragments of data. The approach uses the Minimum Description Length principle for guiding the extraction process that searches for a minimal patterns-set with maximal informativeness. Differently from [7], our approach is concerned with extracting an *exhaustive* set of patterns characterizing a table fragment w.r.t. entire table and a set of attributes.

B. Relative data completeness

Information completeness is a major data quality issue that received attention in the database context [13]–[16]. Several approaches have addressed the problem of assessing the query answer completeness when queries are evaluated on a database with possibly missing tuples or Null values. Relative information completeness assumes the existence of a virtual or materialized reference database DB_C describing the full extent of data. The data set can be described by views over a virtual DB_C [15] and assessing the completeness of a query resorts to determining whether it can be answered using these views. In [17], data completeness is defined by a set of containment constraints between the database D and a master dataset DB_C, and D is complete for a query Q relative to DB_C, if adding tuples to D either violates some constraints or does not change the answer of Q.

The use of metadata for describing the data completeness has been investigated in [13][14][16][18]. *C-tables* [13] and *m-tables* [18] have been proposed for annotating tuples with certainty information and propagating certainty to query answers. In [16], patterns were used to annotate tables with completeness information and a pattern algebra was designed for reasoning on query answer completeness. Differently from [16], which assumes the existence of a set of patterns describing complete data fragments, our approach investigates how to efficiently extract such patterns from reference data and, more importantly, how to ensure that the extracted patterns exhaustively capture completeness information. Moreover, we do not restrict ourselves to the study of completeness but use patterns as means to characterize any data fragment with respect to a reference dataset and a set of attributes.

III. Data Model

In this section, we introduce the notion of fragment summary as a comprehensive description of all complete data categories in a data fragment. Let S and T be two relational tables such that $S \subseteq T$. Then S is called a *fragment* of *source or reference table* T and the pair $F = (S, T)$ is called a *constrained fragment*. For example, any table T with Null values for a given attribute A can be decomposed into two constrained fragments $F_{notnull} = (S_{notnull}, T)$ and $F_{null} = (S_{null}, T)$ where fragment S_{null} contains all tuples in T *with null values for* A and fragment $S_{notnull}$ contains all tuples in T *without null values*. In the following, we assume that the source table T of each constrained fragment is known and use without distinction the terms *fragment* and *constrained fragment*.

A. Fragment Summaries and Patterns

Let $A = \{a_1, a_2, ..., a_n\}$ be a set of attributes where the domain of each attribute is extended by a distinguished *wildcard* value $*$. A *pattern* $p = [a_1 : v_1, a_2 : v_2, ..., a_n : v_n]$ over A is a tuple that assigns to each attribute $a_i \in A$ a value $v_i \in dom(a_i) \cup \{*\}$ in the extended domain of a_i. A set of patterns $P(A) = \{p_1, p_2, \ldots, p_k\}$ over a set of attributes A is called a *pattern table*. We denote by $[*]$ the *wildcard pattern* where all pattern attributes are assigned to wildcards. Observe that a pattern table might contain only data tuples, i.e. patterns without any wildcards.

A pattern table P defines a hierarchy of patterns $L_F = (P^*, \leq)$ where $p \leq p'$ if p can be obtained from p' *by replacing zero or more constants by wildcards* (p is called a specialization of p') and P^* contains all patterns p' such that there exists a pattern $p \in P$ where $p' \leq p$ or $p \leq p'$. Then, the *pattern instance* $\triangleleft(p, S)$ of a pattern p over pattern attributes A in some table S is the sub-fragment or *category* of tuples $t \in S$ where $t[A] \leq p$ ($t[A]$ denotes the projection of t on attributes A). It is also easy to show that the following properties hold for pattern instances:

- $\triangleleft([*], S) = S$;
- $\triangleleft(p, \triangleleft(p, S)) = \triangleleft(p, S)$;
- $S \subseteq S' \Rightarrow \triangleleft(p, S) \subseteq \triangleleft(p, S')$.

The notion of instance can naturally be extended from patterns to pattern tables P and constrained fragments $F = (S, T)$: $\triangleleft(P, S) = \bigcup_{p \in P} \triangleleft(p, S)$ and $\triangleleft(P, F) = (\triangleleft(P, S), \triangleleft(p, T))$.

The following definitions introduce several properties for pattern sets that are necessary for defining the notion of fragment summary. Constrained fragments are related to pattern tables through the notion of *pattern satisfaction*. A constrained fragment $F = (S, T)$ *satisfies* a pattern p if the instance of p in the data table T is equal to the instance of p in the fragment S: $\triangleleft(p, T) = \triangleleft(p, S)$. We also say that pattern p *characterizes* fragment F. By extension, a constrained fragment F *satisfies* a completeness pattern table P if F satisfies all patterns in P. We can show that all fragments F_i in Section I satisfy the corresponding pattern tables P_i. A pattern table P *covers* a constrained fragment F if *for all patterns* p characterizing fragment F, there exists a pattern $p' \in P$ where $p \leq p'$. We can show that all pattern tables P_i in the introduction cover the corresponding fragments F_i. Observe that a pattern table P covering a constrained fragment F is not necessarily satisfied by F. In particular, all pattern table containing the universal pattern cover (but are not satisfied by) *all* constrained fragments. Then, a pattern table P *strictly covers* a constrained fragment F if P covers F and F satisfies P. Finally, a pattern table P is *reduced* if there exists no pair of distinct patterns $p \in P$ and $p' \in P$ such that $p' \leq p$.

Proposition 1: For each constrained fragment F, there exists a unique *reduced strict cover*, called the *fragment summary* of F, and denoted by $\triangleright(F)$.

All pattern tables P_i in the introduction are fragment summaries of the corresponding fragments F_i.

First, observe that a fragment summary $\triangleright(F)$ is not necessarily minimal with respect to instantiation, i.e., there might exist a subset of patterns $P' \subset \triangleright(F)$ where $\triangleleft(P', F) = \triangleleft(\triangleright(F), F)$ (all categories described $\triangleright(F)$ are subsumed by the patterns in P'). This makes our summarization model different from other models, which try to maximize the compression ratio, whereas fragment summaries are compact representations of *all* characteristic data categories. Second, a fragment summary might only cover a strict subset of its fragment $F = (S, T)$, *i.e.*, $\triangleleft(\triangleright(F), T) \subset F[A]$. We call the set of all tuples in $t \in F - \triangleleft(\triangleright(F), T)$ the *rest* of F: $\mathcal{R}(F) = S[A] - \triangleleft(\triangleright(F), F)$. The rest $\mathcal{R}(F)$ defines all categories of tuples in F that cannot be distinguished from other data tuples $t' \notin F$ by pattern attributes A, *i.e.* $t[A] = t'[A]$. This rest can again be considered as a new fragment that can be summarized. We also can easily show that, if A is a key in the source data table T, the rest is empty, *i.e.*, $\triangleleft(\triangleright(F), F) = S[A]$ for all fragments $F = (S, T)$.

IV. Computing Fragment Summaries

Algorithm *FoldData* (Algorithm 1) computes for a given constrained table $F = (S, T)$ a strict cover $\triangleright(F)$ over a set of attributes A. If A is the set of all attributes in F, *FoldData* produces the summary of F. The algorithm explores the data table by searching for complete sub-fragments (categories) that correspond to some specific pattern. It starts from the most general pattern *i.e.* wildcard pattern $[*]$ (level 0) and explores *top-down* and *breadth-first* the pattern subsumption lattice L_S generated by the active attribute domains in the data table S. Each level l corresponds to all patterns p with l constants. For checking if some pattern p is satisfied by S, the algorithm compares the size of the instances in p in S and T. After each level, all specializations of the derived complete patterns p are by definition also complete and the tuples covered by p can be pruned from S before executing the next level. Algorithm $FoldData$ uses the following functions:

- $powerSet(A, level)$ produces all sets of $level$ attributes in A.
- $patterns(A, S)$ produces for a set of attributes A all patterns $\pi_A(S) \times \{[*]\}$
- $checkComp(p, S, T)$ checks if $\lhd(p, S) = \lhd(p, T)$
- $prune(P, S)$ deletes from S all tuples satisfied by patterns $p \in P$.

Observe that operations $checkComp$ and $patterns$ can be implemented by standard SQL queries. In particular, $patterns$ is a simple projection on S and $checkComp$ can be implemented by comparing the result of two $count$-queries on S and T (we suppose that $S \subseteq T$). In the worst case, $FoldData$ explores

Algorithm 1: Algorithm $FoldData$

Data: constrained table $F = (S, T)$, attribute set A
Result: summary $\rhd(F)$
$P := \emptyset$; **for** $level := 0$ **to** $|A|$ **do**
  $\mathcal{X} := \emptyset$;
  for $B \in powerSet(A, level)$ **do**
    for $p \in patterns(B, S)$ **do**
      if $checkComp(p, S, T)$ **then**
        $P := P \cup \{p\}$; $\mathcal{X} := \mathcal{X} \cup \{p\}$;
  $prune(\mathcal{X}, S)$;
return P

(almost) the whole pattern lattice L_S that is generated by all attribute$\times$value combinations in the fragment. The number of patterns $size(L_S)$ of L_S depends on the active attribute domains in the fragment S and the number of attributes $n = |A|$: $size(L_S) = \sum_{i=1}^{n}(C_i^n) * D_i$ where D_i is the maximum size of the Cartesian product of the active domain of i attributes in the data table. The size of the source table influences the cost of checking pattern satisfaction. We also can estimate an upper bound for the fragment summary size as follows. Each tuple in the fragment generates between 0 (for tuples that are subsumed by patterns generated by other tuples) and k patterns, where k is the number of identifiers of the tuple in the source (reference) table. In the worst case, the size of the generated summary is $max_{1 \le i \le n} C_i^n \simeq C_{n/2}^n$ times the size of the fragment where $n = |A|$ is the number of attributes in A. Such a worst-case scenario corresponds to the particular case of random missing data with highly correlated attribute values and no pruning opportunities. If all attributes are necessary to identify any tuple in the source table (independent attribute domains), the fragment summary cannot get bigger than the fragment. As we show in our experiments, real-world data generally follows more regular incompleteness schemes, which increase the compression rate and folding performance.

V. Reasoning with Fragment Summaries

A. Formal reasoning model

Fragment summaries and fragment patterns in general are concise characterizations of data fragments and can be used for analyzing and comparing data fragments extracted from a given reference data set. By the previous definition of fragment summary, the following constraints hold for all constrained fragments $F = (S, T)$ where $T \neq \emptyset$ and all patterns $p \in \rhd(F)$ of their summaries :

- the instance $\lhd(p, S)$ is *complete* with respect to T and *not empty*.
- the instances $\lhd(p', S)$ of all specializations p' of p are complete with respect to T (but might be empty) and
- the instances $\lhd(p', S)$ of all generalizations $p' \neq p$ of p are *incomplete* with respect to T and *not empty*.

Similarly, let $\overline{F} = (\overline{S}, T)$ denote the *complement* of fragment F where $\overline{S}$ contains all tuples "missing" in S w.r.t. T and $\rhd(\overline{F})$ be the summary of $\overline{F}$. Then as before, we can show for all $F = (S, T)$ where $T \neq \emptyset$ and all patterns $p \in \rhd(\overline{F})$ in the summary of $\overline{F}$:

- the instance $\lhd(p, S)$ is *incomplete* with respect to T and *empty*.
- the instances $\lhd(p', S)$ of all specializations p' of p are empty (but might be complete) and
- the instances $\lhd(p', S)$ of all generalization $p' \neq p$ of p are incomplete with respect to T and not empty.

We can show that the rest of a fragment summary is equal to the rest of its complement $\mathcal{R}(\rhd(F)) = \mathcal{R}(\rhd(\overline{F}))$. We denote the summary of this rest of "indistinguishable" patterns by $ND(F, \overline{F}) = \rhd(\mathcal{R}(\rhd(F)) = \rhd(\mathcal{R}(\rhd(\overline{F}))$.

For all patterns p where there exists no generalization in $\rhd(F) \cup \rhd(\overline{F})$ the following holds :

- the intersection between the instance $\lhd(p, F)$ and both, F and $\overline{F}$ is not empty.
- if p is a tuple (only constant attribute values), then p and all generalizations of p are in $ND(F, \overline{F})$.

Based on these properties, all patterns in the summary of a fragment F can be classified into (1) C patterns, which have a complete instance in the fragment, (2) ND patterns, which have a incomplete and *indistinguishable* instance in the fragment, (3) E patterns, which have an empty instance in the source (reference) table and (4) IN patterns, which cover all other patterns. Recall from our introduction example in Section I the "White Male Married" fragment from the Adult dataset. Table III shows some patterns of each fragment summary of fragments "high income", "low income" and "indistinguishable" (ND). For simplification, we assume in the following that these tables represent the entire fragment summaries. Consider the patterns in Table IV. We want to reason and decide for each pattern the fragment belongs to.

Figure 1 is a tree representation of patterns where each node at some level i corresponds to a pattern of length i and each node corresponds to an attribute value at a given level. The wildcard pattern $[*]$ is the root; the first level

TABLE IV. ADULT DATASET PATTERNS

age	workc	education	occupation
*	*	*	*
< 20	*	*	*
40 − 50	*	*	*
*	*	masters	*
*	*	doctorate	*
40 − 50	*	preschool	*
> 60	*	doctorate	*
*	federal-gov	doctorate	*
40 − 50	*	*	Armed-force
40 − 50	never-worked	*	Armed-force

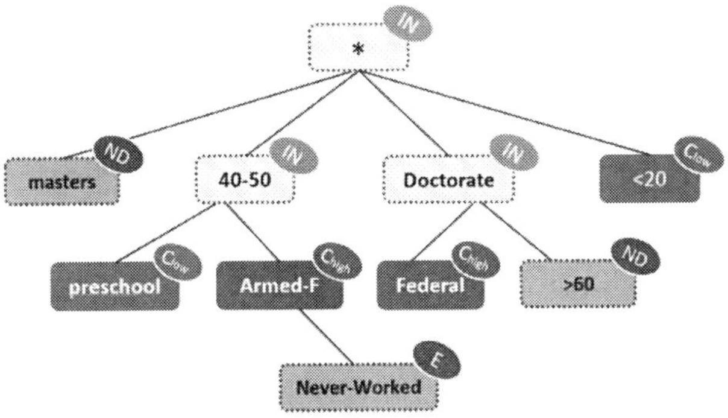

Figure 1. Labeled completeness pattern hierarchy

corresponds to patterns $[*, *, masters, *]$, $[40-50, *, *, *]$, $[*, *, doctorate, *]$ and $[<20, *, *, *]$ with one attribute. The second level specializes the patterns at level one by replacing one wildcard by a constant. All patterns in summary $\triangleright(High)$ are complete and labeled by C_{high} (in blue) and all patterns in summary $\triangleright(Low)$ are labeled C_{low} (in orange). All ancestors of these patterns nodes are IN-patterns (incomplete, not empty, distinguishable). Patterns $[*, *, masters, *]$ and $[>60, *, Doctorate, *]$ are indistinguishable (ND) (in red). Finally, pattern $[40-50, never-worked, *, Armed-Forces]$ is empty (label E) since it specializes a complete high income pattern $[40-50, *, *, Armed-Forces]$ and a complete low income pattern $[*, never-worked, *, *]$ (not shown in Figure 1).

B. Reasoning with SQL Queries

Let $RA_{ext} = RA \cup \{\triangleright, \triangleleft\}$ be the relational algebra extended by two operators $\triangleright$ and $\triangleleft$ where (1) $\triangleleft_A(P)$ generates for a given pattern table P an *equivalent* pattern table P' where all values of attributes $a_i \in A$ are constant values and (2) $\triangleright_A(P)$ generates for a given pattern table P an *equivalent* pattern table where there exists no pattern p and subset $S \subseteq P'$ with more than one pattern that is equivalent to p : $\nexists p, S \subseteq P', |S| > 1 : \{p\} \equiv S$. Using this extended algebra, we can define queries over fragment summaries. First we can define two operators $\triangleright(F) = \triangleright_A(F)$ and $\triangleleft(P) = \triangleleft_A(P)$ that compute the summary of some fragment F and the instance of a pattern table P, respectively. Unfolding $\triangleleft$ can directly be translated into the relational algebra by joining the pattern table with the data table, whereas folding $\triangleright$ over a set of attributes needs recursion, which is not expressible in relational algebra (see Section IV for implementations of $\triangleright$). Based on this formalization, it is then possible to rewrite any pattern query *without folding* into a relational SQL query over source tables and their fragment summaries. We will illustrate this by two examples.

First, selection can be applied for checking if some given pattern p is a specialization/generalization of a pattern $p' \in P$. For example, when considering the summary P in Table IV, pattern $[40-50, *, Doctorate, Armed-Forces]$ is complete (C) in fragment $High$ or empty(E) in the source table if the result of following query over the summary $\mathcal{P}(High)$ is not empty:

```
select * from P(High)
where (age='40-50' or age='*')
and (education='Doctorate' or education ='*')
and (occupation='Armed-Forces' or occupation='*')
```

It is easy to see that the result contains pattern $[40-50, *, *, Armed-Forces]$.

Joining two summaries needs unfolding. Consider two summaries $P_1(age, workc)$ and $P_2(workc, education)$ of two fragments S_1 and S_2 of data table Adult. The natural join of these two summaries generates a new summary $P(age, workc, education)$ characterizing the fragment $S_1 \bowtie S_2$:

```
select P1.age,T.workc,P2.education
from P1, P2, Adult
where (P1.age=Adult.age or P1.age=*)
and (P1.workc=Adult.workc or P1.workc=*)
and (P2.workc=Adult.workc or P2.workc=*)
and (P2.education=Adult.education or P2.education=*)
```

Observe that we have to join both summaries with the data set on attribute $workc$ to filter out all empty result patterns. The resulting pattern table might not be minimal and has to be re-folded over attribute $workc$ to obtain a minimal summary.

VI. EXPERIMENTS

We conducted a set of experiments on two real-life data sets. In each data set, we chose the characteristics that fit a specific use case, in order to evaluate the use and efficiency of our model in a targeted fashion.

A. Completeness summaries for sensor data

The first use case of our study considers a real sensor data set recorded by the network of our university campus. This data set includes measures about various campus resources (lighting, electricity, water, temperature, etc.). We restrict on measures pertaining to temperatures collected in 12 buildings equipped with temperature sensors and refer to this data set with **Temp**.

We build two reference data sets with different spatial coverage and over the same time interval. The first reference, noted $\mathbf{T}_{All}$, includes all spatial locations of the campus regardless of the existence of temperature sensors. The second reference, noted $\mathbf{T}_{Temp}$, restricts on localities equipped with a *temperature* sensor, that is, localities present in **Temp**. The schema of the data and the reference tables are as follows whereas their sizes are reported in Table V.

$\mathbf{Temp}(\underline{building, floor, room, year, month, day, hour}, temp)$
$\mathbf{Loc_x}(\underline{building, floor, room})$ $\mathbf{Cal}(\underline{year, month, day, hour})$

Both reference tables $\mathbf{T}_x$ (where $x = All$ or $x = Temp$) are defined by the Cartesian product of a location table $\mathbf{Loc_x}$ and the same calendar table **Cal** and contain the key of **Temp**.

TABLE V. SIZE OF REFERENCE TABLES $\mathbf{T}_{ALL}$ AND $\mathbf{T}_{TEMP}$

x	$\|Loc_x\|$	$\|Cal_x\|$	$\|\mathbf{T}_x\| = \|Loc_x\| \times \|Cal_x\|$
All	10,757	8,760	94,231,320
Temp	2,810	8,760	24,615,600

1) Complete and missing fragments: In addition to fragment **Temp**, we build two smaller data fragments by restricting **Temp** *spatially* to one building (building 25) and *temporally* to one month (January). The resulting fragments are respectively denoted by **Temp_OneBlg** and **Temp_OneMon**. For each data fragment ds we also define two "narrower" reference data sets $\mathbf{T}^{ds}_{All}$ and $\mathbf{T}^{ds}_{Temp}$ obtained by using same spatial or temporal restriction of ds on reference tables $\mathbf{T}_{All}$ and $\mathbf{T}_{Temp}$.

Complete pattern summaries remain unchanged with the reference extension, but it is more efficient to restrict the study to the areas covered by sensors to avoid producing extra pattern sets (missing summary) and decrease the execution time when producing fragment summaries (see Table VI).

TABLE VI. PATTERN DERIVATION: EXECUTION TIME

data set ds	$\|P(ds)\|$	Execution time (sec)	
		T_Temp	T_All
Temp	$11,269$	$5,983$	$32,620$
Temp_OneBlg	39	45	45
Temp_OneMon	119	75	90

2) Compactness: We measure the effectiveness of patterns in terms of compactness and the efficiency of Algorithm $FoldData$. The *compactness* of a pattern table P is defined by the ratio $|P|/|S|$ between the size of summary P and the size of the data fragment S (low compactness means high compression ratio). We consider for this part the restricted reference T_{Temp} , and report results in table VII.

TABLE VII. PATTERN DERIVATION: PRELIMINARY RESULTS

data set ds	$\|P_C\|$	$\|Comp._C\|$	$\|P_M\|$	$\|Comp_M\|$
Temp	11,269	85×10^{-4}	7,086	2.86×10^{-4}
Temp_OneBlg	39	1.1×10^{-4}	36	0.28×10^{-4}
Temp_OneMon	119	13×10^{-4}	222	1.1×10^{-4}

3) Performance: In the following experiment, we evaluate the performance of algorithm $FoldData$. Table VI reports the execution time for the three data sets and both reference data sets. We notice that the execution time mainly depends on the number of generated patterns and the reference data size and the fragment size itself has a low impact on running time.

To study the evolution of the execution time w.r.t the number of patterns and the fragment size, we derive from the original data fragment **Temp**, 30 sub-fragments grouped into three categories with approximately the same completeness ratio but of different size. Figure 2 shows the running time of $FoldData$ for all fragments according to the number of generated patterns. Points of different colors denote fragments of different size ($orange = 15\%$, $violet = 10\%$ and $green = 3\%$ of the reference data set).

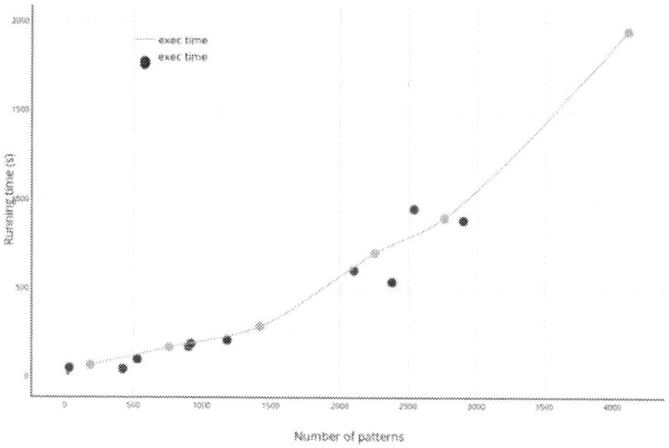

Figure 2. $FoldData$ performance

Notice that execution time is not impacted by the fragment size but grows exponentially with the number of generated patterns.

B. Census income (Adult) data set

The Adult data set is a public data set from the UCI (University of California Irvine) machine learning repository [6], which contains census data about population income. The data set consists of $32,561$ tuples over 14 attributes. For our experiments, we keep a subset of 8 attributes: one numerical attribute, *age* ranging from 17 to 90, and seven categorical attributes: *Workclass* (Private, Federal-Gov...), *Education* (Bachelors, Doctorate,...), *Marital-Status* (Married, Divorced..), *Occupation* (Tech-Support, Sales,...), *Race* (Black, White,...), *Sex* (Female, Male), *Income* ($<$50k,$\geq$50k). This data set is widely used for learning population income classes (high income $>$50K, and low $<=$50k). We achieve different tasks using this data set: 1) completeness/missingness characterization regarding the occupation attribute and 2) income classes summarization.

1) Data completeness analysis: In this data set, *Occupation* and *Workclass* are the only attributes with Null values and generate the same complete and missing fragments with/without Null values. The preliminary results of the completeness analysis are shown in Table VIII.

TABLE VIII. COMPLETENESS AND MISSING PATTERNS FOR OCCUPATION/WORKCLASS

workclass/occupation	complete		missing	
data set	data	patterns	data	patterns
Adult	30718	3363	1843	521

2) Income class summarization: The results are reported in table IX. We can see that by decreasing the number of attributes, the coverage of the corresponding summaries decreases and the size of the rest increases. We also can see that the number of patterns in a summary might be higher than the data set it describes (for example, the summary for high income in $D1$). This is due to the fact that a summary precisely characterizes the fragment with respect to the whole data set and therefore contains more information about the data

TABLE IX. INCOME CLASSES SUMMARIES WITH VARIABLE ATTRIBUTES SETS

		Age : numerical						Age : categorical					
data set	Attributes	High income		Low income		Not distinguishable		High income		Low income		Not distinguishable	
		Data	Patterns	Data	Patterns	Data	Patterns	Data	Patterns	Data	Patterns	Data	Patterns
D_1	Ag,Wo,Ed,MS,Oc,Ra,Se	4382	5485	20848	10924	7544	1995	1591	1813	15227	4096	15743	1454
D_2	Ag,Ed,MS,Oc,Se	2283	1786	18164	4736	12114	1859	394	284	11235	971	20932	736
D_3	Ag,Ed,MS,Oc	1712	1106	16964	3131	13858	1762	184	133	9363	493	23014	645

Ag:age, **Wo**:Workclass, **Ed**:Education,**MS**:Marital-Status,**Oc**:Occupation,**Ra**:Race,Se:Sex

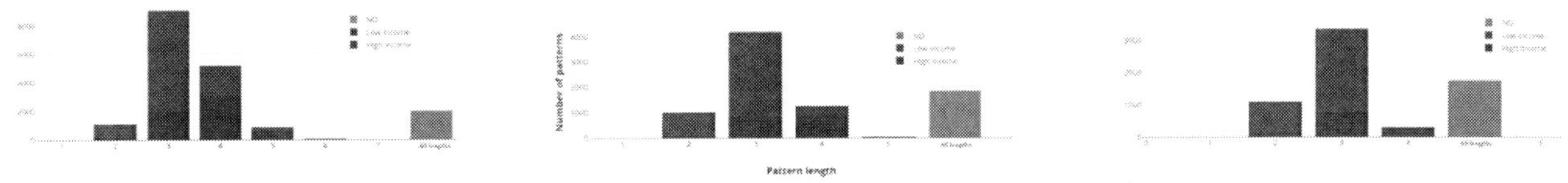

(a) Seven attributes (b) Five attributes (c) Four attributes

Figure 3. Income classes pattern summaries with variable attributes sets (Age as a numerical attribute)

fragment than the fragment itself. The table also shows that reducing the attribute *Age* domain, by aggregating values (numerical to categorical), lead to increasing the size of *ND*, which can be explained by the fine-grained correlation between the Age attribute and the Income. Figure 3 shows the distribution of patterns according to their length (number of constant values in a pattern). For example, in D_2 we infer that 74 patterns of length 2, are in the high-income summary, while $1,033$ belong to low-income summary. This means that for data covered by both patterns sets, we can decide about their income by knowing only two attributes among 7. We also observe the evolution of the size of the pattern set corresponding to non-distinguishable data (in yellow), increasing with attribute set restriction.

The running time increases with the number of attributes. The larger the attribute set is, the more attribute combinations have to be checked during pattern generation. Table X summarizes the running times for fragment *Low* in all data sets.

TABLE X. EXECUTION TIME DEPENDING ON ATTRIBUTES NUMBER

Data set	Number of attributes	Running time (s)
D_1	7	259.19
D_2	5	60.96
D_3	4	32.87

C. Compactness study for synthetic data sets

We showed in previous experiments various results for pattern summary compactness for both data sets (Temp and Adult). While the compactness for complete and missing data fragments summaries over Temp was very low, we can observe in Table IX that high/low-income fragment summaries suffer from a bad compactness, that even exceeds 1 in some cases (D_1: Age numerical : High income). This difference can be explained by the data distribution over the fragments: sensors fail in a continuous time intervals, leading to long complete and incomplete data sequences, which can be summarized by a small number of generic patterns. On the other hand, high and low-income tuples in the Adult data set are distributed in a

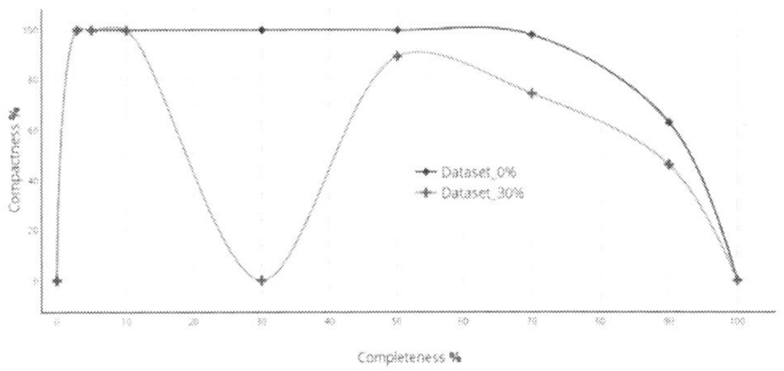

Figure 4. Random evolution

random way over the attributes domains, which leads to large sets of specific patterns. To better understand this phenomena, we created two series of synthetic data sets starting from the **Temp** data set and simulated a set of sensors producing data with different missing/available data distributions.

1) Dense distribution data sets are obtained by sequentially (in time order) adding new measures to T_{Temp}.
2) Sparse distribution data sets are generated by randomly deleting measures from T_{Temp}.

We generate a series of data sets by increasing and decreasing the completeness of three initial data sets with completeness fixed to 0% (empty), 30% and 50% respectively. For each initial data set, we simulate two types of evolution (1) by successively inserting tuples from the reference until reaching full completeness and (2) by successively deleting tuples until reaching emptiness. The insertion and deletions follow two strategies: i) a sequential strategy that selects the (inserted or deleted) tuples using their spatial and temporal domain order preserving the original data distribution and which we call *sequential evolution*, and ii) a random strategy that picks these tuples in a random fashion, we call *random evolution*.

Figures 4 and 5 depict the variation of compactness for each data set and its evolution. In the randomly evolving data

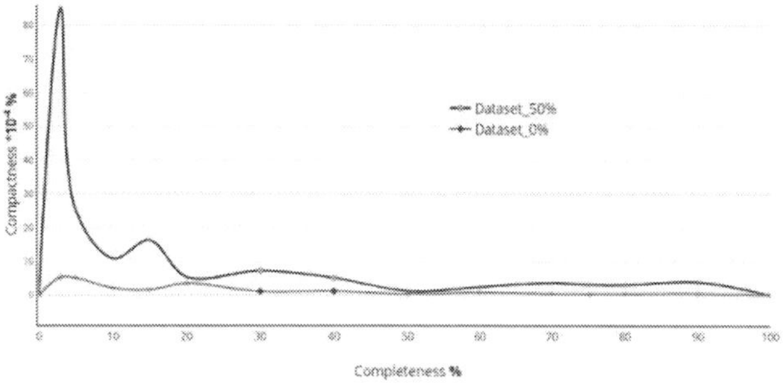

Figure 5. Sequential evolution

sets (Figures 4), the compactness of a random data set with 30% completeness evolves symmetrically in both directions (insertion and deletion). Random insertions and deletions first generate new patterns and cause at some point the fusion of fine-grained patterns to coarser-grained ones to achieve maximum compactness at both extremities. In the sequentially evolving data sets, we observe the same trend with a lower amplitude for a data set with 50% initial completeness: insertions lead to a faster completion of the partial partitions (thanks to order sensitive updates) and thus to faster derivation of coarser patterns without deriving all their subsumed patterns.

VII. Conclusion

We have proposed a formal summarization model and introduced reasoning mechanisms for characterizing the contents of data fragments relative to a complete dataset. We illustrated the use of our framework within two application scenarios for reasoning about information completeness and for characterizing fragment summaries. We have illustrated our approach and validated its implementation experimentally on two data sets. A natural extension under study is the use of Apache Spark [19] for computing and querying summaries for very large fragmented data sets. We also intend to implement a visual query interface for the interactive exploration of fragment summaries.

References

[1] W. A. Voglozin, G. Raschia, L. Ughetto, and N. Mouaddib, "Querying a summary of database," Journal of Intelligent Information Systems, vol. 26, no. 1, Jan. 2006, pp. 59–73.

[2] F. Buccafurri, F. Furfaro, D. Sacca, and C. Sirangelo, "A Quad-tree Based Multiresolution Approach for Two-dimensional Summary Data," in Proceedings of the 15th International Conference on Scientific and Statistical Database Management, ser. SSDBM '03. Washington, DC, USA: IEEE Computer Society, 2003, pp. 127–140.

[3] A. Cuzzocrea and D. Sacc, "H-IQTS: A Semantics-aware Histogram for Compressing Categorical OLAP Data," in Proceedings of the 2008 International Symposium on Database Engineering & Applications, ser. IDEAS '08. New York, NY, USA: ACM, 2008, pp. 209–217.

[4] H.-J. Lenz and A. Shoshani, "Summarizability in OLAP and statistical data bases," in Scientific and Statistical Database Management, 1997. Proceedings., Ninth International Conference on. IEEE, 1997, pp. 132–143.

[5] L. V. Lakshmanan, J. Pei, and J. Han, "Quotient cube: How to summarize the semantics of a data cube," in Proceedings of the 28th international conference on Very Large Data Bases. VLDB Endowment, 2002, pp. 778–789.

[6] "Adult income dataset," Accessed on March 2019, https://archive.ics.uci.edu/ml/index.php.

[7] J. Chen, J.-Y. Pan, C. Faloutsos, and S. Papadimitriou, "TSum: fast, principled table summarization," in Proceedings of the Seventh International Workshop on Data Mining for Online Advertising - ADKDD '13. Chicago, Illinois: ACM Press, 2013, pp. 1–9.

[8] G. Raschia and N. Mouaddib, "SAINTETIQ: a fuzzy set-based approach to database summarization," Fuzzy sets and systems, vol. 129, no. 2, 2002, pp. 137–162.

[9] R. Saint-Paul, G. Raschia, and N. Mouaddib, "General Purpose Database Summarization," in Proceedings of the 31st International Conference on Very Large Data Bases, ser. VLDB '05. Trondheim, Norway: VLDB Endowment, 2005, pp. 733–744.

[10] M.-L. Lo, K.-L. Wu, and P. S. Yu, "Tabsum: A flexible and dynamic table summarization approach," in Distributed Computing Systems, 2000. Proceedings. 20th International Conference on. IEEE, 2000, pp. 628–635.

[11] M. van Leeuwen and J. Vreeken, "Mining and Using Sets of Patterns through Compression," in Frequent Pattern Mining, C. C. Aggarwal and J. Han, Eds. Cham: Springer International Publishing, 2014, pp. 165–198.

[12] A. Koopman and A. Siebes, "Characteristic Relational Patterns," in Proceedings of the 15th ACM SIGKDD International Conference on Knowledge Discovery and Data Mining, ser. KDD '09. New York, NY, USA: ACM, 2009, pp. 437–446.

[13] T. Imieliński and W. Lipski, "Incomplete information in relational databases," in Readings in Artificial Intelligence and Databases. Elsevier, 1988, pp. 342–360.

[14] A. Motro, "Integrity = Validity + Completeness," ACM Trans. Database Syst., vol. 14, no. 4, Dec. 1989, pp. 480–502.

[15] A. Y. Levy, "Obtaining Complete Answers from Incomplete Databases," in Proceedings of the 22th International Conference on Very Large Data Bases, ser. VLDB '96. San Francisco, CA, USA: Morgan Kaufmann Publishers Inc., 1996, pp. 402–412.

[16] S. Razniewski, F. Korn, W. Nutt, and D. Srivastava, "Identifying the extent of completeness of query answers over partially complete databases," in Proceedings of the 2015 ACM SIGMOD International Conference on Management of Data, Melbourne, Victoria, Australia, May 31 - June 4 2015, pp. 561–576.

[17] W. Fan and F. Geerts, "Relative Information Completeness," ACM Trans. Database Syst., vol. 35, no. 4, Oct. 2010, pp. 27:1–27:44.

[18] B. Sundarmurthy, P. Koutris, W. Lang, J. F. Naughton, and V. Tannen, "m-tables: Representing missing data," in 20th International Conference on Database Theory, ICDT, Venice, Italy, March 2017, pp. 21:1–21:20.

[19] M. Zaharia et al., "Apache spark: a unified engine for big data processing," Communications of the ACM, vol. 59, no. 11, 2016, pp. 56–65.

A Context Data Metamodel for Distributed Middleware Platforms in Smart Cities

Júlio Suzuki Lopes
Federal Institute of Paraíba (IFPB)
João Pessoa, Brazil
email: julio.lopes@ifpb.edu.br

Lucas Vale F. da Silva, Gledson Elias
Federal University of Paraíba (UFPB)
João Pessoa, Brazil
email: lucasfaustino@ppgi.ci.ufpb.br, gledson@ci.ufpb.br

Abstract—**The concept of smart cities is related to the development of services, systems and applications to provide sustainable solutions for a huge and fast-growing population in urban areas. In a smart cities context, the wide range of application domains leads to a variety of large independent local repositories with non-unified data models that support very limited interoperability and, more importantly, hinder data reuse, integration, extension and partitioning. In order to address such issues, this paper presents a metamodel for specification and instantiation of context data in smart cities driven by interoperable distributed middleware platforms, enabling data integration, reuse, extension and partitioning, supplied by several independent data providers across a lot of application domains. Supported by an experimental prototype implementation, empirical results based on a semi-real dataset evince the potential benefits and practical applicability of the proposed metamodel.**

Keywords-smart cities; context modeling; context-awareness; data integration and partitioning.

I. INTRODUCTION

The concept of smart cities has gained a lot of attention from researchers around the world [1]. The core of this concept has explored the fact that the adoption of ICTs (Information and Communication Technologies) can improve quality of life and mitigate urban issues resulted from rapid population growth [2]. Among such ICTs, IoT (Internet of Things) is a key technology to solve major problems faced by people living in cities, enabling a range of services and applications by interconnecting digital and physical things (e.g., smartphones, TVs, vehicles) to share data and resources [3].

Nowadays, in large cities, a number of services, systems and applications have been developed with focus on specific urban problem domains, for instance, traffic and waste management, smart health and smart education [4]. Most of such software solutions are developed and managed by several public or private stakeholders, which adopt different ICT platforms and infrastructures [5], leading to a variety of large independent, local repositories with non-unified data models [6] and segmented data [5], resulting in the formation of the *information island* phenomenon [7]. Consequently, current solutions for smart cities support very limited interoperability and, more importantly, hinder data integration, reuse, extension and partitioning.

As a means to avoid information islands, in a way similar to the concept of virtual data warehouses [8], one of the main challenges in distributed middleware platforms for smart cities is to find a way to provide an integrated view of big urban data, enabling the development of interoperable services, systems and applications that communicate with each other for creating holistic and contextualized views of the cities [9][10].

In such a scenario, the adoption of a unified data model plays an important role, acting as a kind of glue that can bind services, systems and applications together. However, a unified data model for data integration is not enough. Regarding the dynamic, elastic and changeable nature of big urban data, such a unified data model ought also to facilitate data reuse, extension and partitioning.

In order to address such issues, this paper presents a metamodel for specification and instantiation of context data associated to all kinds of entities in smart cities. More importantly, the proposed metamodel, called DCDS (*Distributed Context Data Schema*), can be adopted as a unified data model in interoperable distributed middleware platforms for enabling data integration, reuse, extension and partitioning, supplied by several independent data providers across a lot of application domains. Supported by an experimental prototype implementation, empirical results based on a semi-real dataset evince the potential benefits and practical applicability of the proposed metamodel.

The remainder of the paper is structured as follows. Section 2 identifies the requirements related to data models for smart cities. Then, Section 3 discusses some related work, highlighting how identified requirements are handled by each one. Section 4 presents the proposed metamodel, detailing how to create schemas and instances related to smart cities entities, whose context data can be integrated, reused, extended and partitioned. Next, Section 5 shows a use case based on a large semi-real dataset on public urban transport. Concluding, Section 6 presents some final remarks, limitations and future work.

II. REQUIREMENTS FOR SMART CITIES DATA MODELS

This section identifies some requirements for data models that aim to ease the development of interoperable services, systems and applications in the smart cities scenario. To do that, an initial list of requirements has been derived through a literature review, covering a reasonable set of studies and proposals [11]-[20]. Note that the goal is not to be comprehensive, but rather to provide an overview of the main requirements. Accordingly, the conducted literature review has identified the following requirements:

- **Flexibility** – enables easy adaptation to different smart cities contexts, being not bounded to a single application or even a specific domain [13].
- **Expressivity** – concerned with the generic problem of knowledge representation [11], ensures a wide data design space for specification and instantiation of several data types related to smart cities entities.
- **Simplicity** – adopts a minimal number of structuring, composition and control rules, making more intelligible and easier data modelling processes [12].
- **Semanticability** – attaches semantic annotations as a means to enable human or automatic inspection and transformation of context data in heterogeneous distributed shared scenarios [14][15].
- **Granularability** – represents the characteristics of the context data at different levels of detail [13], including composite entities, structured datatypes and partial attribute assignments.
- **Interoperability** – supports structured unambiguous schemas to define entities and their attributes [17], which are helpful in data exchange among heterogeneous distributed platforms.
- **Reusability** – boosted also by structured schemas that act as reusable data contracts, encouraging to develop data-driven services in which ecosystem's actors can publish and share reusable datasets [18].
- **Integrability** – represents a step beyond reuse, in which ecosystem's actors can integrate other different external datasets, providing added value services or adapting to different target purposes [18].
- **Extensibility** – allows schemas and their associated instances to evolve over time and accommodate changes readily, dealing with the inherent diversity and dynamism of smart cities [19].
- **Partitionability** – enables context data related to smart cities entities to be partitioned or splitted up in multiple hosting nodes [20], supporting concurrent access to increase performance and scalability [16].

III. RELATED WORK

Data models have been proposed for platforms, systems, services and applications in several smart cities contexts. However, most of them have been adopted in centralized approaches, in which a single module, service, repository or node, herein called broker, is responsible for storing and managing the whole urban data, which obviously do not scale very well. Inversely, the proposed metamodel can be adopted in distributed approaches, in which multiple brokers can store context data related to smart cities entities in a distributed and even partitioned manner.

Based on XML (Extensible Markup Language), *ContextML* (CML) is a language designed by the C-Cast project [21] and adopted in the IoT architecture proposed by Cippra [22]. In both, it has been adopted as a common representation for exchanging context data between their respective components. Thus, it defines a markup language for context representation and mainly communication that should be supported by all components of compliant architectures. As a result, CML can meet the interoperability requirement, however, has a not so simple syntax. Note that the C-Cast project [21] and the Cippra architecture [22] propose centralized approaches that do not deal with issues related to partitionability.

Other two projects, *SENSEI* [23] and *IoT-A* [12], define data models to provide interoperability. Context entities are called resources in SENSEI and virtual entities in IoT-A. In both, the respective data models allow to represent real-world entities making possible to be aware of the context or environment in which such entities operate or can be accessed. Due to that, SENSEI and IoT-A can adequately meet the expressivity requirement, however, do not adopt a simple way to represent such entities, requiring expertise in low-level protocols, device standards and data formats. As a result, the effort for modelling entities is quite high and full of challenges even in simple cases. Despite that, both projects propose methods to orchestrate IoT services in order to combine together several resources or virtual entities in different granularities, providing high-level services based on semantic and ontological concerns.

NGSI (Next Generation Service Interfaces) [24][25] defines a context management information model that adopts the concept of entities as virtual representation of all kinds of real-world physical objects. In NGSI, each entity has a state represented by attributes, providing context-awareness in a simple, flexible and expressive way to compliant platforms and applications [12][24]. Despite defining mechanisms to manage references to external entities [25], in essence, NGSI presupposes the adoption of centralized approaches in compliant middleware platforms. As a result, a reasonable effort is required to explore partitioned context data among multiple brokers, imposing an issue related to scalability.

Based on the requirements identified for smart cities data models, Table I contrasts CML, SENSEI, IoT-A, NGSI and the proposed DCDS metamodel. The comparison takes as a starting point the evaluation presented by Jara *et al.* [12] and Nitti *et al.* [26] but enriched with new requirements and proposals. In all cases, the evaluated proposals were analyzed based on a set of concepts, properties and observations, directly extracted by us from their respective documentations. In Table I, note that the conducted evaluation adopts black dots to represent the degree of attendance for each proposal with respect to each requirement, varying from zero to three dots.

TABLE I. SMART CITY DATA MODELS

	CML	SENSEI	IoT-A	NGSI	DCDS
Flexibility	•••	•••	•••	•••	•••
Expressivity	•••	•••	•••	•••	•••
Simplicity	•	•	•	•••	•••
Semanticability	•	•••	•••	••	••
Granularability	•	••	••	••	•••
Interoperability	••	••	••	••	•••
Reusability	•	••	••	••	•••
Integrability	•	••	••	••	•••
Extensibility	•••	••	••	••	•••
Partitionability	-	-	-	•	•••

As can be observed in Table I, among related work, NGSI has higher levels of attendance for almost all requirements, representing a promising data model to deal with smart cities entities. In fact, due to that, some existing projects have adopted the NGSI model, including the *Fiware* platform [27] that has gained a lot of attention in smart cities research communities. Despite that, as can be noticed, NGSI has limitations related to granularability, reusability, integrability, extensibility and partitionability. Regarding that smart cities scenarios require the ability to deal with massive urban data produced by a very large number of data sources and providers, such NGSI limitations have direct and strong impact on compliant smart cities platforms in respect to their scalability, usability and so practical applicability. Acting as a complementary approach, taking NGSI capabilities as a basis, the proposed DCDS metamodel introduces some simple but key additional features in order to better deal with several issues related to granularability, reusability, integrability, extensibility and partitionability.

IV. A Distributed Context Data Schema

In order to improve existing proposals for smart cities data models, this section presents a context data metamodel, called DCDS, which provides the means to specify and instantiate context information associated to all kinds of real-world entities in a broad range of smart cities domains. As the main benefits and contributions, DCDS can be adopted as a unified data model in interoperable distributed middleware platforms for enabling data integration, reuse, extension and partitioning, supplied by several independent data providers across a lot of application domains. The remainder of this section describes the DCDS metamodel in more depth, including how to specify and instantiate smart cities entities, and how to support data partitioning.

A. *Specifying and Instantiating Entities*

DCDS adopts the concepts of *entity schema* and *entity instance* for representing the unambiguous single specification and the multiple associated instances for each context entity, respectively. Using UML (Unified Modeling Language), as illustrated in Figure 1, the representation of an *entity schema* has four constituting model elements.

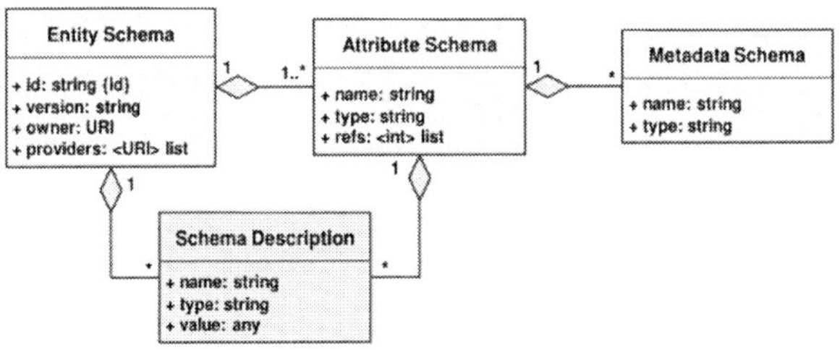

Figure 1. DCDS UML representation.

As the starting point of an entity schema, the *Entity Schema* model element has the following terms: ***id*** – provides a globally unique identifier for each entity schema; ***version*** – indicates the version of the respective entity schema, enabling providers to manage the entity schema lifecycle; ***owner*** – identifies the owner/provider that has specified the entity schema, allowing all providers to share schemas among them; and ***providers*** – defines a list of multiple providers in which related instances of the entity schema can be integrally or partially stored and retrieved.

Each context entity can have several context attributes, each one represented in the respective schema by the *Attribute Schema* model element, which has the following terms: ***name*** – provides a unique identifier for each attribute associated to the given entity schema; ***type*** – indicates the type of the respective attribute (e.g., string, integer and float); and ***refs*** – defines a list of references to providers in which the given attribute can be stored and retrieved. Note that, as explained later, the terms *providers* and *refs* are the basis for two distinct data partitioning types, which in turn leverage data granularity in an innovative way.

The other two model elements *Metadata Schema* and *Schema Description* are related to different types of optional metadata, which can be adopted to enrich information about schemas and instances, varying among simple textual descriptions, rich semantic annotations, and well-known adopted metrics, patterns and even standards. On the one hand, *Metadata Schema* denotes different types of metadata that can be associated to the given attribute during the instantiation of context entities. On the other hand, *Schema Description* represents metadata descriptions that can be associated to the specification of the own schema and the respective attributes. Each *Metadata Schema* and *Schema Description* model element has two terms, ***name*** and ***type***, providing a unique identifier for each metadata and indicating the type of the given metadata, respectively. Besides, each *Schema Description* has the ***value*** term for representing the specific metadata content.

Based on entity schemas, DCDS provides a simple, flexible and expressive way to describe unambiguous context entities in smart cities scenarios. As another important feature, each entity schema can be evaluated by compliant parsers and even engines to syntactically and semantically validate distributed context entity data, making possible to interoperate and integrate reusable context data managed by different providers in smart cities scenarios.

A step further, versioned schemas leverage extensibility, enabling to evolve context entity specifications and their instances over time, accommodating changes as a means to deal with the dynamic nature of urban data. For instance, new attributes and metadata can be included in schemas and subsequently their instances. Besides, already existing attributes and metadata can be renamed, updated or even removed. Therefore, it is possible to support CRUD (Create, Read, Update and Delete) operations for context entity schemas and instances. More importantly, such operations can also be employed in the list of providers where related instances and their attributes can be integrally or partially stored and retrieved. Of course, a compliant platform ought to define an API (Application Programming Interface) for dealing with the extensibility related to entity schemas and their attributes.

In practice, the DCDS UML representation must be converted to a context representation language. Among existing languages, for instance XML, CSV (Comma-Separated Values) and RDF (Resource Description Framework), JSON (JavaScript Object Notation) [28] has gained more and more attention in IoT scenarios, since it is simpler, smaller, faster and more readable than XML [29]. Figure 2 shows an example of a DCDS JSON schema.

```
{
"id":"bus",
"version":"1.0",
"owner":"dcds.provider1.br",
"providers":["dcds.provider1.br", "dcds.provider2.br", "dcds.provider3.br"],
"schema-description":{
   "description":{
      "type":"text",
      "value":"Buses of the public transport system"}},
"location":{
   "type":"point",
   "refs":[1, 2],
   "schema-description":{
      "format":{
         "type":"text",
         "value":"GeoJson georeferenced location"}}},
"speed":{
   "type":"double",
   "refs":[1, 3],
   "metadata-schema":{
      "unit":{
         "type":"string"}}},
"people-ammount":{
   "type":"integer",
   "refs":[1, 2, 3]}
}
```

Figure 2. DCDS JSON schema representation.

In smart cities platforms, systems and applications, each real-world physical entity (e.g., sensors, actuators, automobiles and users) can be modeled and represented as a virtual context entity, which is denoted as an *entity instance* in the DCDS metamodel. Using a UML representation, as illustrated in Figure 3, an entity instance has three constituting model elements. Note that each entity instance must be compliant with its respective entity schema. As such, an entity instance can only have attributes and metadata previously specified in its corresponding entity schema.

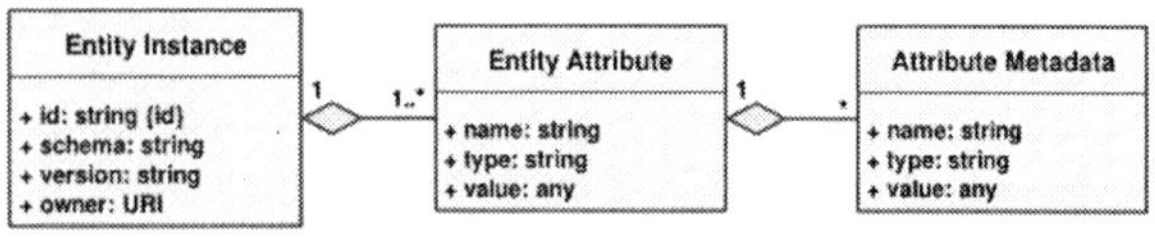

Figure 3. Context entity UML model.

Acting as the starting point of an entity instance, the *Entity Instance* model element has the following terms: ***id*** – provides a local identifier for each entity instance from the producer viewpoint; ***schema*** – indicates the compliant entity schema that defines the context information for the respective type of entity instance; ***version*** – denotes the version of the respective entity schema; ***owner*** – identifies the owner/provider that specified the compliant entity schema. Note that, together, the terms *id, schema, version* and *owner* provide a globally unique identifier for each entity instance, enabling compliant middleware platforms to provide naming services to leverage location transparency for schemas and their respective instances.

Each entity instance can have several context attributes, each one represented in the respective entity instance by the *Entity Attribute* model element, which has the following terms: ***name*** – denotes the attribute name defined in the corresponding entity schema; ***type*** – indicates the type of the respective attribute (e.g., string, integer and float); and ***value*** – represents the current value of the attribute in the given entity instance. In order to provide high granularity levels, a compliant middleware platform must have the capability of storing and retrieving integrally or partially the attributes of managed entity instances.

As specified in an entity schema, each entity instance can have optional associated metadata for providing contextual information about the given attribute instance. To do that, DCDS adopts the *Attribute Metadata* model element, which has three terms, ***name***, ***type*** and ***value***, denoting respectively the metadata name, type and specific content, all of them defined in the associated entity schema.

Figure 4 illustrates a simple example of a DCDS JSON instance, compliant with the DCDS JSON schema previously defined in Figure 2. As can be noticed, DCDS defines a context information model similar to NGSI [24] but enriched with the concept of entity schemas for leveraging the support to the identified requirements.

```
{
"id":"CT01-1 Circular-Tourism",
"schema":"bus",
"version":"1.0",
"owner":"dcds.provider1.br",
"location":{
   "type":"point",
   "value":[30.52, 10.25]},
"speed":{
   "type":"double",
   "value":60.35,
   "unit":{
      "type":"string",
      "value":"kilometer per hour - km/h"}},
"people-ammount":{
   "type":"integer",
   "value":32}
}
```

Figure 4. DCDS JSON instance representation.

In order to provide a formal DCDS representation, EBNF (Extended Backus-Naur Form) grammars have been specified for entity schemas and instances, making possible to develop DCDS parsers. Due to space limitations and for the sake of simplicity, Figure 5 illustrates the EBNF grammar for entity schemas only, but without including the *Schema Description* model element.

```
dcds_schema ::= '{' entity_schema (',' attribute_schema)+ '}'

entity_schema ::= '"id":' '"' string '"' ','
                  '"version":' '"' string '"' ','
                  '"owner":' '"' uri '"' ','
                  '"providers":' '[' uri (',' uri)* ']'

attribute_schema ::= attribute_spec (',' metadata_schema)*

attribute_spec ::= '"' attr_name '"' ':' '{'
                   '"type":' '"' string '"' ','
                   '"refs":' '[' integer (',' integer)* ']'
                   '}'

metadata_schema ::= '"metadata-schema:"' '{'
                       '"' meta_name '"' ':' '{'
                          '"type":' '"' string '"' '}'
                    '}'

attr_name ::= string
meta_name ::= string
```

Figure 5. EBNF grammar for DCDS schemas.

B. Partitioning Context Instances and Attributes

Based on the DCDS metamodel, compliant middleware platforms can provide data partitioning in a two-fold perspective: *context instance partitioning* and *context attribute partitioning*. Such partitioning perspectives have a direct influence on requirements related to integrability, granularability and reusability, making possible services, systems and applications to integrate reusable context data from multiple providers in different granularity levels. Figure 6a and Figure 6b depict both partitioning approaches.

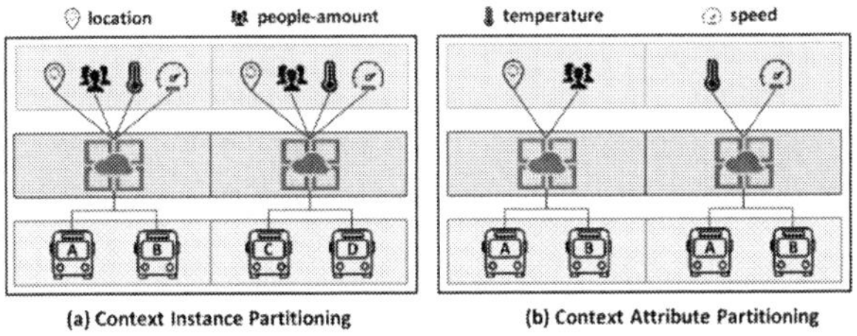

Figure 6. Data partitioning approaches.

In the *context instance partitioning* (Figure 6a), multiple independent data providers can store and manage subsets of entity instances related to the same entity schema. Thus, instead of storing the whole set of entity instances in a single provider, subsets of them are partitioned in multiple providers based on organizational, economical or geographical policies. Note that, for each entity instance, all currently valued attributes of the instance are integrally stored in a single provider, but without the need of assigning values to all attributes.

For example, in large cities, where there can be several bus operator companies responsible by providing the public transportation system, it sounds interesting that every company stores and manages context data about its own bus fleet. Figure 6a presents an example of instance partitioning, in which two providers manage all context data (*location*, *people-amount*, *speed* and *temperature*) associated with the bus fleet of two independent bus operator companies, which have the buses A/B and C/D, respectively. To do that, the ***providers*** term of the respective entity schema must simply include the URI (Uniform Resource Identifier) list of the authorized providers. Figure 7 illustrates the instance representation for buses A and C, which are integrally stored in different data providers with all attributes.

```
{
"id":"Bus-A",
"schema":"bus",
"version":"1.0",
"owner":"dcds.provider1.br",
"location":{
    "type":"point",
    "value":[-23.56, -46.65]},
"speed":{
    "type":"double",
    "value":60.35},
"people-ammount":{
    "type":"integer",
    "value":32},
"temperature":{
    "type":"double",
    "value":22.25}
}
```

```
{
"id":"Bus-C",
"schema":"bus",
"version":"1.0",
"owner":"dcds.provider1.br",
"location":{
    "type":"point",
    "value":[-50.12, -18.20]},
"speed":{
    "type":"double",
    "value":25.35},
"people-ammount":{
    "type":"integer",
    "value":10},
"temperature":{
    "type":"double",
    "value":19.00}
}
```

Figure 7. Instance partition example.

Differently, in the *context attribute partitioning* (Figure 6b), multiple independent data providers can store and manage subsets of attributes related to the same type of entity instances. That is, instead of storing all attributes of a given entity instance in a single provider, subsets of them are partitioned in multiple providers, probably based on expertise and capabilities of such providers. Again, there is no need of assigning values to all attributes.

For instance, in several cities, where the public transportation system is only provided by the municipal government, it seems interesting to hire distinct specialized companies for gathering and managing different context data types of interest. Figure 6b shows an example of attribute partitioning, in which two providers separately manage two distinct context attributes (*location/people-amount* and *speed/temperature*) associated with the municipal bus fleet. To do that, similarly, the ***providers*** term of the target entity schema must have the URI list of the authorized providers; but differently, for each attribute, the ***refs*** term must have the ordinal positions in the URI list of the providers that can store the respective attribute. Figure 8 illustrates the instance representation for bus A, which are partially stored in two different data providers without the need of assigning values to all attributes in each provider.

```
{
"id":"Bus-A",
"schema":"bus",
"version":"1.0",
"owner":"dcds.provider1.br",
"location":{
    "type":"point",
    "value":[-23.56, -46.65]},
"people-ammount":{
    "type":"integer",
    "value":32}
}
```

```
{
"id":"Bus-A",
"schema":"bus",
"version":"1.0",
"owner":"dcds.provider1.br",
"speed":{
    "type":"double",
    "value":25.35},
"temperature":{
    "type":"double",
    "value":19.00}
}
```

Figure 8. Attribute partition example.

In order to manage both partitioning perspectives, a compliant DCDS provider ought to adopt an integration process for combining all required instances associated to a given schema, version and provider. In the *context instance partitioning*, the requesting provider has to retrieve partial collections of instances stored in different providers and thereafter to integrate all them to provide the whole set of required instances. In the *context attribute partitioning*, the same process must be performed but, additionally, the requesting provider has to concatenate partial attributes of instances retrieved from different providers to reconstruct the whole set of attributes for all required instances.

It is important to emphasize that, in case of relational storage, both partitioning perspectives can be mapped to horizontal and vertical partitioning, as indicated in [30] for RDBMS (Relational Database Management Systems). In such a case, on the one hand, the *context instance partitioning* can be mapped to the *horizontal partitioning*, in which context instances are partitioned into disjoint sets of rows that are physically stored and accessed separately in different RDBMS-based providers. On the other hand, the *context attribute partitioning* can be mapped to the vertical partitioning, in which context attributes are partitioned into disjoint sets of columns that are physically stored and accessed separately in different RDBMS-based providers.

V. EXPERIMENTAL EVALUATION

In order to evaluate DCDS, based on HTTP (Hypertext Transfer Protocol) and REST (Representational State Transfer), a prototype implementation of a compliant distributed middleware platform, called *Sirius*, has been developed as a set of RESTful services for integrating multiple data providers, supporting the development of services, systems and applications in a broad range of smart cities domains.

As illustrated in Figure 9, *Sirius* adopts a service-oriented architecture. The *Context Schema Manager* deals with the versioned lifecycle of entity schemas, including CRUD operations for schemas and their respective attributes and metadata. Taking such specified schemas as a basis, the *Context Instance Manager* coordinates communication among other distributed *Sirius* brokers for storing, retrieving and integrating instances, including CRUD operations for instances and their respective attributes and metadata. By implementing a query processor, the *Context Query Engine* deals with a simple query language that can be adopted to transparently access and integrate context data from multiple providers. In order to provide independence from low-level database technologies, each *Context Broker Adapter* acts as a translator among DCDS JSON representations and a given low-level representation model. Therefore, several *Context Broker Adapters* can provide a way to map or transform different structured or unstructured data models into DCDS schemas.

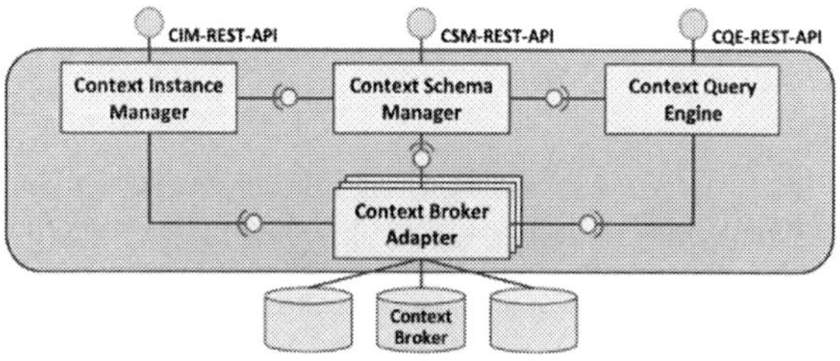

Figure 9. Sirius middleware platform.

Sirius was developed using *Flask*, a lightweight Python microframework for developing web applications and RESTful services. In addition, *Sirius* adopts *Orion Context Broker* [31] as a local broker for persisting instances. In order to define a distributed platform, virtual machines deployed in the AWS (Amazon Web Services) cloud infrastructure [32] act as context providers, running complete *Sirius* platform instances.

In the DCDS experimental evaluation, a semi-real dataset is adopted, taking as a basis the real-time database of the urban transport system provided by the São Paulo town hall in Brazil. Such a database provides an HTTP RESTful API to access the real-time context data related to all bus fleets provided by bus operator companies in São Paulo. Originally, the context database provides information related to the name of the line, location and travel direction of about 10,000 buses. However, for enriching the context attributes associated to buses, the conducted experiments have included additional synthetic attributes. Thus, in the bus schema, each bus instance has the following attributes: *location*, *people-amount*, *temperature* and *speed*.

In a way similar to Figure 6a and Figure 6b, two different experiments have been successfully evaluated using six virtual machines in the AWS cloud infrastructure, four of them to deploy *Sirius* instances, another one to deploy *Orion* and the last one to use as a client to dispatch operations. In the first experiment, the *context instance partitioning* approach was evaluated, spreading 10,000 bus instances in four *Sirius* brokers, which means around 2,500 bus instances in each broker. In such a case, each bus instance has all four attributes stored in the respective broker. In the second experiment, the *context attribute partitioning* approach was evaluated, storing all 10,000 bus instances repeatedly in each *Sirius* broker. However, differently, each bus instance has only one attribute stored in each *Sirius* broker. As a mean to define a comparing baseline, the experiment also has a third configuration in which all buses are stored a centralized *Orion* broker.

As an initial performance evaluation, a configurable set of concurrent users, varying from 10 to 100, dispatch read requests for each configuration of the experiment, each one recovering the whole set of 10,000 stored instances. Then, for each set of concurrent users, the total time for processing such requests was measured. The experiment was conducted using the *JMeter* load testing tool [33], which allows to configure different load profiles and calculate their respective response times for a variety of services. In *JMeter*, HTTP requests can be modeled as users, which perform concurrent requests to target services.

Figure 10 shows the total response time for each configuration (*instance partitioning*, *attributed partitioning* and *centralized Orion*) and the set of concurrent users (*10, 20, 40, 60, 80, 100*). Of course, the lower the response time, the better performance has the evaluated configuration.

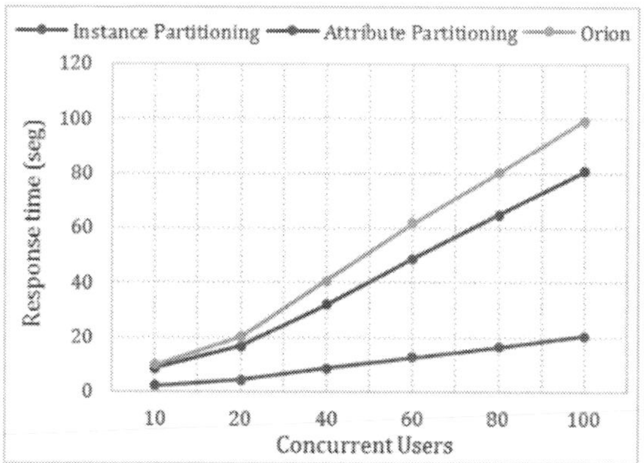

Figure 10. Performace evaluation.

As can be noticed, in both partitioning configurations, as the number of concurrent users increases, the *Sirius'* distributed approach provides better and better performance when contrasted with the *Orion's* centralized approach. For example, considering 100 concurrent users, the gains of the instance and attribute partitioning approaches are around 79.4% and 18.9%, respectively.

VI. Conclusion and Future Work

In order to evolve from not so scalable, centralized smart cities platforms, this paper presents the DCDS metamodel, which provides a means to specify and instantiate distributed, partitioned and versioned context information associated to all kinds of real-world entities in a broad range of smart cities domains. As the main contributions, DCDS can be adopted as a unified data model in interoperable, scalable and distributed middleware platforms, enabling the development of services, systems and applications that can easily deal with capabilities related to data integration, reuse, extension and partitioning, supplied by several independent providers across a lot of smart cities domains.

On the one hand, in DCDS, versioned schemas and instances enable to evolve entity schemas and their instances over time, accommodating changes imposed by dynamic urban data. On the other hand, DCDS enables data partitioning in an innovative two-fold approach. First, multiple providers can manage subsets of instances related to the same schema. Second, multiple providers can manage subsets of attributes related to the same type of instances. As contributions, such versioning and partitioning capabilities leverage requirements related to extensibility, integrability, granularability and reusability, enabling services, systems and applications to integrate reusable, extensible context data from multiple providers in distinct granularity levels.

It is important to highlight that both partitioning approaches have the potential to provide better response time and scalability in compliant middleware platforms due to gains imposed by parallel access [16], concentrating frequently accessed instances or attributes in providers with more available or less overloaded processing power, communication bandwidth and storage capacity.

Despite such contributions, from the viewpoint of complaint platforms, DCDS does not have concerns related to security requirements, such as access control, authentication, confidentiality and denial of service. Besides, in collaborative distributed smart cities initiatives, business models ought to be adopted in order to regulate how to monetize data providers. Together, concerns related to security and business models represent key potential branches for future work.

As another future branch, it is important to conduct performance, load and stress tests with much bigger scenarios, including a lot of data provider nodes and several types of context entities in different smart cities domains. Such tests enable to gather more confidence about empirical findings related to enumerated requirements of interest, but also including scalability and availability.

References

[1] T. Nam and T. A. Pardo, "Conceptualizing Smart City with Dimensions of Technology, People, and Institutions", 12th Int. Conf. on Digital Government Research, 2011, pp. 282-291.

[2] H. Chourabi, *et al.*, "Understanding Smart Cities: An Integrative Framework", 45th Hawaii Int. Conf. on Syst. Sci., 2012, pp. 2289-2297.

[3] E. Borgia, "The Internet of Things Vision: Key Features, Applications and Open Issues", Computer Commun., vol. 54, pp. 1-31, Dec. 2014.

[4] M. Naphade, G. Banavar, C. Harrison, J. Paraszczak, and R. Morris, "Smarter Cities and their Innovation Challenges", Computer, Issue 6, pp. 32-39, Jun. 2011.

[5] N. Ben-Sassi, *et al.*, "Service Discovery and Composition in Smart Cities", Int. Conf. on Adv. Inf. Syst. Eng., 2018, pp. 39-48.

[6] A. J. Jara, *et al.*, "Smart Cities Semantics and Data Models", Int. Conf. on Inf. Technol. & Syst., 2018, vol. 721, pp. 77-85.

[7] F. J. Villanueva, M. J. Santofimia, D. Villa, J. Barba, and J. C. Lopez, "Civitas: The Smart City Middleware from Sensors to Big Data", 7th Int. Conf. on Innovative Mobile and Internet Serv. in Ubiquitous Comput., 2013, pp. 445-450.

[8] M. Crowe, C. Begg, F. Laux, and M. Laiho, "Data validation for big live data", 9th Int. Conf. on Advances in Databases, Knowl., and Data Appl., 2017, pp. 30-36.

[9] I. A. Hashem, *et al.*, "The Role of Big Data in Smart City", Int. J. of Inf. Manag., vol. 36, n. 5, pp. 748-758, Oct. 2016.

[10] M. Strohbach, H. Ziekow, V. Gazis, and N. Akiva, "Towards a Big Data Analytics Framework for IoT and Smart City Applications", In: F. Xhafa, L. Barolli, A. Barolli, and P. Papajorgji (eds), Modeling and Processing for Next-Generation Big-Data Technologies, vol 4, pp. 257-282, 2015.

[11] P. Bellavista, A. Corradi, M. Fanelli, and L. Foschini, "A Survey of Context Data Distribution for Mobile Ubiquitous Systems", ACM Comput. Surveys, vol. 44, n. 4, pp. 24-28, Aug. 2012.

[12] A. J. Jara, *et al.*, "Semantic Web of Things: An Analysis of the Application Semantics for the IoT Moving Towards the IoT Convergence", Int. J. of Web and Grid Serv., vol. 10, n. 2/3, pp. 244-272, Apr. 2014.

[13] C. Bolchini, C. A. Curino, E. Quintarelli, F. A. Schreiber, and L. Tanca, "A Data-Oriented Survey of Context Models", ACM SIGMOD Record, vol. 36, n. 4, pp. 19-26, Dec. 2007.

[14] R. Reichle, *et al.*, "A Comprehensive Context Modeling Framework for Pervasive Computing Systems", Int. Conf. on Distrib. Appl. and Interoperable Syst., vol.5053, 2008, pp. 281-295.

[15] A. J. Jara, Y. Bocchi, D. Fernandez, G. Molina, and A. Gomez, "An Analysis of Context-Aware Data Models for Smart Cities: Towards Fiware and ETSI CIM Emerging Data Model", Int. Archives of Photogrammetry, Remote Sens. and Spatial Inf. Sci., vol. XLII-4/W3, pp. 43-50, Set. 2017.

[16] M. Boussard, *et al.*, "A Process for Generating Concrete Architectures", Enabling Things to Talk, Springer, pp. 45-111, 2013.

[17] W. C. McGee, "On User Criteria for Data Model Evaluation", ACM Trans. on Database Syst., vol. 1, n. 4, pp. 370-387, 1976.

[18] A. A. García, M. O. U. Criado, and C. P. Heredero, "The Ecosystem of Services around Smart Cities: An Exploratory Analysis", Procedia Comput. Sci., vol. 64, pp. 1075-1080, 2015.

[19] J. Lee, S. Baik, and C. C. Lee, "Building an Integrated Service Management Platform for Ubiquitous Ecological Cities", Computer, vol. 44, n. 6, pp. 56-63, 2011.

[20] R. White and J. Tantsura, "Navigating Network Complexity: Next-Generation Routing with SDN", Service Virtualization, and Service Chaining, Addison-Wesley, 2015.

[21] M. Knappmeyer, S. L. Kiani, C. Fra, B. Moltchanov, and N. Baker, "ContextML: A Light-Weight Context Representation and Context Management Schema", 5th Inter. Symp. on Wireless Pervasive Comput., 2010, pp. 367-372.

[22] M. R. Crippa, "Design and Implementation of a Broker for a Service-Oriented Context Management and Distribution Architecture", Undergraduate Thesis, UFRGS, Jul. 2010.

[23] V. Tsiatsis, *et al.*, "The SENSEI Real World Internet Architecture", In: Towards the Future Internet: Emerging Trends from Europe Research, pp. 247-256, 2010.

[24] OMA, "NGSI Context Management", version 1.0, May 2012.

[25] OMA, "NGSI Registration and Discovery", version 1.0, May 2012.

[26] M. Nitti, V. Pilloni, G. Colistra, and L. Atzori, "The Virtual Object as a Major Element of the Internet of Things: A Survey", IEEE Commun. Surveys & Tuts., vol. 18, n. 2, pp. 1228-1240, Nov. 2016.

[27] Fiware, http://www.fiware.org [retrieved: April, 2019].

[28] JSON, http://www.json.org [retrieved: April, 2019].

[29] S. Zunke and V. D'Souza, "JSON vs XML: A Comparative Performance Analysis of Data Exchange Formats", Int. J. of Comp. Sci. and Netw., vol. 3, n. 4, pp. 257-261, Aug. 2014.

[30] S. Agrawal, V. Narasayya, and B. Yang, "Integrating vertical and horizontal partitioning into automated physical database design", Int. Conf. on Manag. of Data, 2004, pp. 359-370.

[31] Orion, http://fiware-orion.readthedocs.io [retrieved: April, 2019].

[32] AWS, http://aws.amazon.com/pt/ec2 [retrieved: April, 2019].

[33] JMeter, http://jmeter.apache.org [retrieved: April, 2019].

Strongly Possible Keys in Incomplete Databases with Limited Domains

Munqath Alattar

Department of Computer Science and
Information Theory
Budapest University of Technology and Economics
Budapest, Hungary
Email: m.attar@cs.bme.hu

Attila Sali

Alfréd Rényi Institute of Mathematics
Hungarian Academy of Sciences
Budapest, Hungary
Email: sali.attila@renyi.mta.hu

***Abstract*—Missing values that may occur in the key attributes of a database table is an extensive problem and handling it is an important and challenging task, as the records need to contain distinct and total values in their key part. The existing effective approaches include an imputation operation for each occurrence of a null in the key part of the data. In this paper, we assume the situation when the attributes domains are not known. For that, a new concept of keys called *strongly possible keys* in databases with null values is introduced. It lies between possible keys and certain keys introduced by Köhler et. al. earlier. The definition uses only information extractable from the database table. Furthermore, an approximation concept of the strongly possible key is provided.**

Keywords–Strongly possible keys; null values; approximation of keys.

I. Introduction

A basic approach to treat null values in keys of relational databases is an imputation operation for each occurrence of a null in the key part of the data with a value from the attribute domain as explained by [1]. We investigate the situation when the attributes' domains are not known. For that, we only consider what we have in the given data and extract the values to be imputed from the data itself for each attribute so that the resulting complete dataset after the imputation would not contain two tuples having the same value in their key. Köhler et al. [1] used possible worlds by replacing each occurrence of a null with a value from the corresponding attribute's (possibly infinite) domain. They defined a possible key as a key that is satisfied by some possible world of a non total database table and a certain key as a key that is satisfied by every possible world of the table. In many cases, we have no proper reason to assume existence of any other attribute value than the ones already existing in the table. Such examples could be types of cars, diagnoses of patients, applied medications, dates of exams, course descriptions, etc. We define a strongly possible key as a key that is satisfied by some possible world that is obtained by replacing each occurrence of null value from the corresponding attribute existing values. We call this kind of a possible world a strongly possible world. This is a data mining type approach; our idea is that we are given a raw table with nulls and we would like to identify possible key sets based on the data only.

The remainder of the paper is organized as follows. In Section 2, some definitions are stated. In Section 3, strongly possible keys, their discovery, and characterization of the implication problem of systems of strongly possible keys are provided. Approximation measures are studied in Section 4. Section 5 presents concluding remarks and future research directions.

II. Definitions

Let $R = \{A_1, A_2, \dots A_n\}$ be a relation schema. The set of all the possible values for each attribute $A_i \in R$ is called the domain of A_i and referred as $D_i = dom(A_i)$ for i = 1,2,... n. And if $X \subseteq R$ then $D_X = \prod_{\forall A_i \in K} D_i$. An instance $T = (t_1, t_2, \dots t_s)$ over R is a set of tuples that each tuple is a function $t : R \to \bigcup_{A_i \in R} dom(A_i)$ and $t[A_i]$ is in the $dom(A_i)$ for all A_i in R. For a tuple $t_r \in T$, let $t_r[A_i]$ be the restriction of the rth tuple of T to A_i.

In practice, data models may contain an unknown information about the value of some tuple $t_j[A_i]$ for j = 0,1,... s that is denoted by $\perp$. t_1 and t_2 are *weakly similar* on $X \subseteq R$ denoted as $t_1[X] \sim_w t_2[X]$ as defined by Köhler [1] if:

$$\forall A \in X \quad (t_1[A] = t_2[A] \text{ or } t_1[A] = \perp \text{ or } t_2[A] = \perp)$$

Furthermore, t_1 and t_2 are *strongly similar* on $X \subseteq T$ denoted by $t_1[X] \sim_s t_2[X]$ if:

$$\forall A \in X \quad (t_1[A] = t_2[A] \neq \perp)$$

For the sake of convenience, we write $t_1 \sim_w t_2$ if t_1 and t_2 are weakly similar on R and the same for strong similarity. For a null-free table, a set of attributes $K \subset R$ is a *key* if there are no two distinct tuples in the table that share the same values in all the attributes of K:

$$t_a[K] \neq t_b[K] \ \forall\ 0 \leq a, b \leq s \text{ such that } a \neq b$$

The concepts of possible and certain keys were defined by Köhler et al [1]. Let $T' = (t'_1, t'_2, \dots t'_s)$ be a table that represents a total version of T which is obtained by replacing the occurrences of $\perp$ in all attributes $t[A_i]$ with a value from the domain D_i different from $\perp$ for each i. T' is called a *possible world* of T. In a possible world T', t'_i is weakly similar to t_i and T' is completely null-free table. A *possible key* K denoted as $p\langle K\rangle$, is a key for some possible world T' of T, so that:

$$t'_1[K] \neq t'_2[K], \ \forall t'_1, t'_2 \in T'$$

Similarly, a *certain key* K referred as $c\langle K\rangle$, is a key for every possible world T' of T. The *visible domain* of an attribute A (VD_A) is the set of all distinct values except $\perp$ that are already used by tuples in T:

$$VD_i = \{t[A_i] : t \in T\} \backslash \{\perp\} \text{ for } A_i \in R$$

The term visible domain refers to the data that already exist in a given dataset. For example, if we have a dataset with no information about the attributes' domains definitions, then we use the data itself to define their own structure and domains. This may provide more realistic results when extracting the relationship between data so it is more reliable to consider only what information we have in a given dataset.

A possible world T' is called *strongly possible world* if $T' \subseteq VD_1 \times VD_2 \times \ldots \times VD_n$.

A subset $K \subseteq R$ is a *strongly possible key* (in notation $sp\langle K\rangle$) in T if $\exists$ a strongly possible world $T' \subseteq VD_1 \times VD_2 \times \ldots \times VD_n$ such that K is a key in T'.

III. RESULTS

Table I implies $sp\langle AB\rangle$ as a strongly possible key because there is a strongly possible world in Table II where AB is a key. On the other hand, Table I implies neither $sp\langle AC\rangle$ nor $sp\langle BC\rangle$ because there is no strongly possible world T' that has AC or BC as keys.

TABLE I. A DATASET WITH NULLS

A	B	C	D
3	2	⊥	0
15	1	2	10
⊥	2	2	⊥

TABLE II. A STRONGLY POSSIBLE WORLD OF TABLE I

A	B	C	D
3	2	2	0
15	1	2	10
15	2	2	10

Let Σ be a set of strongly possible keys and θ a single strongly possible key over a relation schema R. Σ logically implies θ, denoted as $\Sigma \models \theta$ if for every instance T over R satisfying every strongly possible key in Σ we have that T satisfies θ.

Theorem 1: $\Sigma \models sp\langle K\rangle \iff \exists Y \subseteq K$ s.t. $sp\langle Y\rangle \in \Sigma$.

Proof: $\Leftarrow$: $\exists T'$ s.t. $t'_i[Y] \neq t'_j[Y], \forall i \neq j$, so $t'_i[K] \neq t'_j[K], \forall i \neq j$ holds, as well.

$\Rightarrow$: Suppose indirectly that $sp\langle Y\rangle \notin \Sigma\ \forall Y \subseteq K$. Consider the following instance consisting of two tuples $t_1 = (0, 0, \ldots, 0)$, $t_2[K] = (\perp, \perp, \ldots, \perp)$, and $t_2[R \setminus K] = (1, 1, \ldots 1)$ as in Table III . Then, the only possible t'_2 in T' is $t'_2(0, 0, \ldots, 0, 1, 1, \ldots, 1)$. Furthermore, $\forall Z$ where $sp\langle Z\rangle \in \Sigma$, there must be $z \in Z \setminus K$, thus $t'_1[Z] \neq t'_2[Z]$ but $t'_1[K] = t'_2[K]$ showing that (t_1, t_2) satisfies every strongly possible key constraints from Σ, but does not satisfy $sp\langle K\rangle$. ■

TABLE III. INCOMPLETE DATA INSTANCE

	K	$R \setminus K$
t_1	0 0 0 0	00000000
t_2	⊥⊥⊥⊥	11111111

Note 1: If $\Sigma \models \neg sp\langle K\rangle$ and $Y \subseteq K$ then $\Sigma \models \neg sp\langle Y\rangle$.

Note 2: If $\Sigma \models sp\langle K\rangle$, then $\Sigma \models p\langle K\rangle$ but the reverse is not necessarily true, since $D_K \supseteq VD_K$ could be proper containment so K could be made a key by imputing values from $D_K \setminus VD_K$. For example, in Table III, it is shown that $\neg sp\langle K\rangle$ holds, but $p\langle K\rangle$ may hold in some T' if there is at least one other value in the domain of K rather than the zeros to be placed instead of the nulls in the second tuple so that $t'_1[K] \neq t'_2[K]$ results.

Note 3: If $\Sigma \models c\langle K\rangle$, then $\Sigma \models sp\langle K\rangle$. As certain keys hold in any possible world, they hold also if this possible world is created using visible domain.

Note 4: For a single attribute A, $sp\langle A\rangle \iff t[A] \not\sim_w t'[A]\ \forall t, t'$ s.t. $t \neq t'$, i.e., if there are no nulls occurrences in A.

In other words, a single attribute with a null value cannot be a strongly possible key. That is because replacing an occurrence of null with a visible domain value results in duplicated values for that attribute.

Let us consider a schema $R = \{A_1, A_2, \ldots, A_n\}$ and let $\mathcal{K} = \{K_1, K_2, \ldots K_p\}$ be a collection of attribute sets and $T = \{t_1, t_2, \ldots, t_s\}$ be an instance with possible null occurrences. Our main question here is whether $\Sigma = \{sp\langle K_1\rangle, sp\langle K_2\rangle, \ldots, sp\langle K_p\rangle\}$ holds in T? Let $E_i = \{t' \in VD_1 \times VD_2 \times \ldots \times VD_n : t' \sim_w t_i\}$. Let $S \subseteq VD_1 \times VD_2 \times \ldots \times VD_n$ be the union $S = E_1 \cup E_2 \cup \ldots \cup E_s$ and define bipartite graph $G = (T, S; E)$ by $\{t, t'\} \in E \iff t \sim_w t'$ for $t \in T$ and $t' \in S$. Let $(S, \mathcal{M}_0)$ be the transversal matroid (see [2]) defined by G on S, that is a subset $X \subseteq S$ satisfies $X \in \mathcal{M}_0$ if X can be matched into T. Furthermore, consider the partitions

$$S = S_1^j \cup S_2^j \cup \ldots \cup S_{p_j}^j \quad (1)$$

induced by K_j for $j = 1, 2, \ldots, p$ such that S_i^j's are maximal sets of tuples from S that agree on K_j. Let $(S, \mathcal{M}_j)$ be the partition matroid given by (1). We can formulate the following theorem.

Theorem 2: Let T be an instance over schema $R = \{A_1, A_2, \ldots, A_n\}$ and let $\mathcal{K} = \{K_1, K_2, \ldots K_p\}$ be a collection of attribute sets. $\Sigma = \{sp\langle K_1\rangle, sp\langle K_2\rangle, \ldots, sp\langle K_p\rangle\}$ holds in T if and only if the matroids $(S, \mathcal{M}_j)$ have a common independent set of size $|T|$ for $j = 0, 1, \ldots p$

Proof: An independent set T' of size $|T|$ in matroid $(S, \mathcal{M}_0)$ means that tuples in T' form a strongly possible world for T. That they are independent in $(S, \mathcal{M}_j)$ means that K_j is a key in T', that is $sp\langle K_j\rangle$ holds.

Conversely, if $\Sigma = \{sp\langle K_1\rangle, sp\langle K_2\rangle, \ldots, sp\langle K_p\rangle\}$ holds in T, then there exists a strongly possible world $T' = \{t'_1, t'_2, \ldots, t'_s\} \subseteq VD_1 \times VD_2 \times \ldots \times VD_n$ such that $t_i \sim_w t'_i$. This means that $T' \subseteq S$ and that T' is independent in transversal matroid $(S, \mathcal{M}_0)$. $sp\langle K_j\rangle$ holds implies that tuples t'_i are pairwise distinct on K_j, that is T' is independent in partition matroid $(S, \mathcal{M}_j)$. ■

Unfortunately, Theorem 2 does not give a good algorithm to decide the satisfaction of a system Σ of strongly possible keys, because as soon as Σ contains at least two constraints, then we would have to calculate the size of the largest common independent set of at least three matroids, known to be an NP-complete problem [3].

In case of a single strongly possible key $sp\langle K\rangle$ constraint, Theorem 2 requires to compute the largest common independent set of two matroids, which can be solved in polynomial time [4]. However, we can reduce the problem to the somewhat simpler problem of matchings in bipartite graphs.

If we want to decide whether $sp\langle K\rangle$ holds or not, we can forget about the attributes that are not in K since we need distinct values on K as a matching from $VD_{A_1}\times VD_{A_2}\times\ldots\times VD_{A_b}$ to $T=\{t_1,t_2\ldots t_r\}|_K$ where $K=\{A_1,A_2\ldots A_b\}$. Thus, we may construct a table T' that is formed by finding all the possible combinations of the visible domains of $T|_K$ that are weakly similar to some tuple in $T|_K$.

$$T'=\{t':\exists t\in T: t'[K]\sim_w t[K]\}\subseteq VD_1\times VD_2\times\ldots\times VD_b$$

Finding the matching between T and T' that covers all the tuples in T (if it exists) will result in the set of tuples in T' that needs to be replaced in T so that K is a strongly possible key.

Let $c_v(A)$ denote the number of tuples that have value v in attribute A, that is $c_v(A)=|\{t\in T\colon t[A]=v\}|$. Next are some necessary conditions to have a strongly possible key.

Proposition 1: Let $K\subseteq R$ be a set of attributes. If $sp\langle K\rangle$ holds, then

1) No two tuples t_i, t_j are strongly similar in K.
2) $|T|\leq \prod_{\forall A\in K}|VD_A|$.
3) $\forall B\in K$, number of nulls in $B\leq \sum_{\forall v\in VD_B}\left(\frac{\prod_{\forall A\in K}|VD_A|}{|VD_B|}-c_v(B)\right)$.
4) For all $v\in VD_B$ we have $c_v(B)\leq\frac{\prod_{\forall A\in K}|VD_A|}{|VD_B|}$

Proof: The first condition is obviously required so that K is a strongly possible key, where the strong similarity means that the two tuples are total and equal to each other in the key part and this violates the general key definition. In addition to that, for any set of attributes, the maximum number of distinct combination of their values is the size of the multiplication of their visible domain, and this proves (2). Moreover, to prove conditions (3) and (4), when K is $sp\langle K\rangle$ in T then there should exist a T' with no two tuples having the same values in all K attributes after filling all their nulls. So for each set of tuples S that has the same value v in the attribute B, the number of distinct combinations of the other attributes is the multiplication of their VD's, means the number of tuples in S should not be more than $\prod_{\forall A\in(K\setminus B)}VD_A$. Thus, the number of times value v can be used to replace a null in attribute B is at most $\frac{\prod_{\forall A\in K}|VD_A|}{VD_B}-c_v(B)$. ■

Note that $sp\langle K\rangle$ holds if a matching covering T exists in the bipartite graph $G=(T,T';E)$ defined as above, $\{t,t'\}\in E\iff t[K]\sim_w t[K]'$. We can apply Hall's Theorem to obtain

$$\forall X\subseteq T,\text{ we have } |N(X)|\geq|X|$$

$$\text{for } N(X)=\{t'\colon\exists t\in X\text{ such that } t[K]'\sim_w t[K]\}$$

IV. Strongly Possible Keys Approximation

To measure the degree of how much a strongly possible key holds in a given dataset, we use the g_3 measure introduced in [5]. g_3 is based on the idea that the degree to which ASP key is approximate is determined by the minimum number of tuples that need be removed from T so that K becomes an ASP key. To find the tuples that we need to remove, we suggest to construct the maximum matching in graph $G=(T,T';E)$.

$$g_3(K)=\frac{|T|-\nu(G)}{|T|}$$

where $\nu(G)$ denotes the maximum size of a matching in graph G.

Let $\mathcal{M}$ be the collection of connected components in graph G that hold the strongly possible key condition, i.e., there is a matching cover all T tuples in that set ($\forall_{M\in\mathcal{M}}\ \nexists X\subseteq M\cap T$ such that $|X|>N(X)$). Let $C\subseteq G$ be defined as $C=G\setminus\bigcup_{\forall M\in\mathcal{M}}M$ and let $\mathcal{M}'$ be the set of connected components of C. In addition to that, we use the term V_M to denote the set of vertices of T in a component M. So, the maximum matching can be written as $\sum_{M\in\mathcal{M}}(|V_M|)+\sum_{\forall M'\in\mathcal{M}'}\nu(M')$. Therefore we can reformulate the g_3 measure as:

$$g_3(K)=\frac{|T|-(\sum_{M\in\mathcal{M}}(|V_M|)+\sum_{M'\in\mathcal{M}'}\nu(M'))}{|T|}$$

Figure 2 shows 7 tables that represent the key part only of the data where each table has more than one attribute. Tables A, B and C have $2n$ tuples, tables E and F have n tuples, and table D has $n+l$ tuples while table G has kn tuples. Table D includes a variable $0\leq\beta\leq\frac{n}{2}$. We intend to use these cases to illustrate the differences and give a bound of g_3/g_3^c where it is always true that $g_3-g_3^c\geq 0$. The graphs show the weak similarity relationship between the data tuples and the visible domains combinations. The visible domains combinations are shown on Figure 1. For example, in table A, the first two tuples of T in the left side of the graph can have a unique weakly similar tuples in T' for each, while for the rest, every two tuples in T form a connected component that have only one weakly similar tuple in T'. On other hand, all the tuples of table E form connected component of size n that have a weakly similar relation (matching) to one tuple in T'.

Measuring the strongly possible keys approximation can be more appropriate by take into consideration the effect of each connected component in the graph on the matching. More specifically, $\mathcal{M}$ represents the sets of tuples that do not require any tuple to be removed to get a strongly possible key, while the components of $\mathcal{M}'$ represent the sets of tuples that contain some tuples which need to be removed to have a strongly possible key. We consider the components of $\mathcal{M}$ to get their effect doubled in the approximation measure because they represent a part of the data that is not affected by any tuples removal. So, we propose a derived version of g_3 measure named g_3^c that considers the effects of these components.

$$g_3^c(K)=\frac{|T|-(\sum_{M\in\mathcal{M}}(|V_M|)+\sum_{M'\in\mathcal{M}'}\nu(M'))}{|T|+\sum_{M\in\mathcal{M}}|V_M|}$$

Theorem 3: For any table T and set of attributes K we have either $g_3(K)=g_3^c(K)$ or $1<g_3(K)/g_3^c(K)<2$. Furthermore, for any rational number $1\leq\frac{p}{q}<2$ there exist tables of arbitrarily large number of tuples with $g_3(K)/g_3^c(K)=\frac{p}{q}$.

Proof: $g_3(K)$ and $g_3^c(K)$ are different only in the denominator part. The number of tuples of the components in $\mathcal{M}$ can't be more than the total number of tuples in the table, so $0\leq\sum_{M\in\mathcal{M}}|V_M|\leq|T|$ and $\sum_{M\in\mathcal{M}}|V_M|=|T|$ iff every

(A)	$t'_i = (i-1, 0)$ $i = 1, 2, \ldots, n+1$
(B)	$t'_i = (i-1, 0)$ $i = 1, 2, \ldots, n+1$
(C)	$t'_i = (i-1, 0)$ $i = 1, 2, \ldots, n+1$
(D)	$t'_i = (i, 0, 0)$ for $i = 1, 2, \ldots, n-\beta$, and $t'_{n-\beta+j} = (0, 0, j-1)$ for $j = 1, 2, \ldots, l+1$
(E)	$t'_1 = (0, 0)$
(F)	$t'_i = (i, 0)$ $i = 1, 2, \ldots, n-1$
(G)	$t'_{jn+i} = (jn+i+j, 0)$ for $i = 1, 2, \ldots, n-j-1$ and $j = 0, 1, \ldots, k-1$

Figure 1. Visible Domains Combinations of Tables of Figure 2

tuple is a member of some connected component in $\mathcal{M}$. In the latter case $g_3(K) = g_3^c(K)$, otherwise the denominator of $g_3^c(K)$ is less than twice the denominator of $g_3(K)$ that proves the inequlaties of the ratio. Table E proves that $g_3(K) = g_3^c(K)$ can hold for arbitrarily large tables. Now let $1 < \frac{p}{q} < 2$ be given with $\frac{p}{q} = 1 + \frac{p'}{q'}$. Consider Table D where

$$g_3(K)/g_3^c(K) = \left(\frac{\beta-1}{n+l}\right) / \left(\frac{\beta-1}{n+2l}\right)$$

which can simply be written as $1 + \frac{l}{n+l}$. Now taking $n = \alpha(q'-p')$, $l = \alpha p'$ and any β between 2 and $\lfloor \frac{n}{2} \rfloor$ we obtain that

$$g_3(K)/g_3^c(K) = 1 + \frac{p'}{q'}.$$

■

Note that $g_3(K)$ ranges between $1/n$ and $1/2$ depending on the choice of β.

V. Conclusion and Future Directions

The main contributions of this paper are as follows:

- We introduced and defined strongly possible keys over database relations that contain some occurrences of nulls.
- We provided some properties, observations, and number of necessary conditions so that a strongly possible key holds in a given dataset. We show that deciding whether a given set of attributes is a strongly possible key can be done by application of matchings in bipartite graph, so Hall's condition is naturally applied.
- We showed that deciding whether a given system of sets of attributes is a system of possible keys for a given table can be done using matroid intersection. However, we need at least three matroids, and matroid intersection of three or more matroids is NP-complete, which suggests that our problem is also NP-complete.
- We studied systems of strongly possible keys and we gave characterization of the implication problem.
- An approximation concept of the strongly possible key was introduced to measure how close approximation of a strongly possible key holds in a data relation, using g_3 measure. We derived the measure g_3^c from g_3 and gave bounds of the two measures.

Strongly possible keys are special cases of possible keys of relational schemata with each attribute having finite domain. So, future research is needed to decide what properties of implication, axiomatization of inference remain valid in this setting. Note that the main results in [1] consider that at least one attribute has infinite domain.

We plan to extend our research from keys to functional dependencies. Weak and strong functional dependencies were introduced in [6]. A wFD $X \to_w Y$ holds if there is a possible world T' that satisfies FD $X \to Y$, while sFD $X \to_s Y$ holds if every possible world satisfies FD $X \to Y$. Our strongly possible world concept naturally induces an intermediate concept of functional dependency. Future research on possible keys of finite domains might extend our results on strongly possible keys.

Finally, Theorem 2 defines a matroid intersection problem. It would be interesting to know whether this particular question is NP-complete, which we strongly believe it is.

References

[1] H. Köhler, U. Leck, S. Link, and X. Zhou, "Possible and certain keys for sql," The VLDB Journal, vol. 25, 2016, pp. 571–596.

[2] D. Welsh, Matroid Theory. Academic Press, New York, 1976.

[3] M. Garey and D. Johnson, Computers and Intractability. A Guide to the Theory of NP-Completeness. Freeman, New York, 1979.

[4] E. Lawler, "Matroid intersection algorithms," Mathematical Programming, vol. 9, 1975, pp. 31–56.

[5] J. Kivinen and H. Mannila, "Approximate inference of functional dependencies from relations," Theoretical Computer Science, vol. 149, 1995, pp. 129–149.

[6] G. L. Mark Levene, "Axiomatisation of functional dependencies in incomplete relations," Theoretical Computer Science, vol. 206, 1998.

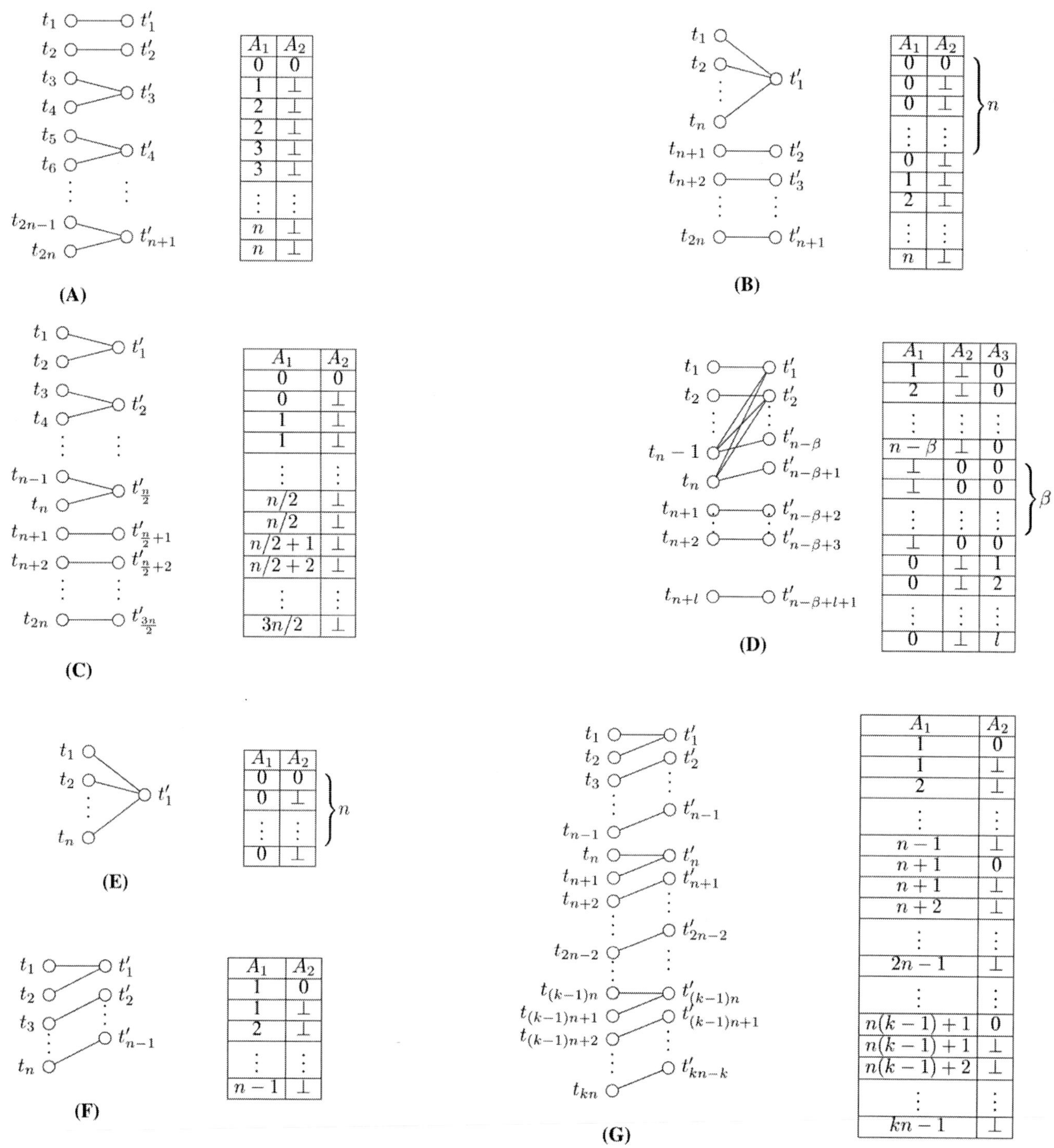

Figure 2. Sample Tables for Comparison Results

TABLE IV. MAIN COMPARISON RESULTS

	A	B	C	D	E	F	G
g_3	$\frac{n-1}{2n}$	$\frac{n-1}{2n}$	$\frac{1}{4}$	$\frac{\beta-1}{n+l}$	$\frac{n-1}{n}$	$\frac{1}{n}$	$\frac{1}{n}$
g_3^c	$\frac{n-1}{2n+2}$	$\frac{n-1}{3n}$	$\frac{1}{6}$	$\frac{\beta-1}{n+2l}$	$\frac{n-1}{n}$	$\frac{1}{2n-2}$	$\frac{1}{2n-2}$

A Skyline Query Processing Approach over Interval Uncertain Data Stream with K-Means Clustering Technique

Zarina Dzolkhifli, Hamidah Ibrahim, Fatimah Sidi, Lilly Suriani Affendey, Siti Nurulain Mohd Rum
Faculty of Computer Science and Information Technology
Universiti Putra Malaysia
Malaysia
e-mail: {zarinadzol@gmail.com, hamidah.ibrahim, fatimah, lilly, snurulain}@upm.edu.my

Ali Amer Alwan
Kulliyyah of Information and Communication Technology,
International Islamic University Malaysia
Malaysia
e-mail: aliamer@iium.edu

***Abstract*—Skyline query processing which extracts a set of interesting objects from a potentially large multidimensional dataset has attracted significant research attention in many emerging important applications. Although skyline computation has been studied extensively for data streams, there has been relatively less work on uncertain data stream. Only recently, a few methods have been proposed to process uncertain data stream, however data uncertainty in these works is restricted to objects having many instances. In contrast, there is no work that has considered uncertainty due to objects having interval values wherein the exact values of the objects are not known at the point of processing. Hence, in this paper a skyline query processing approach utilising the K-Means clustering technique is proposed to efficiently compute skyline over interval uncertain data stream.**

Keywords-skyline query processing; uncertain data; data stream.

I. Introduction

Nowadays, real-time data streams processing technologies play an important role in enabling time-critical decision making in many applications. Handling streaming data is particularly challenging since it is continuously generated by an array of sources and devices and is delivered in a wide variety of formats. The abundance of data streams has led to new algorithmic paradigms for processing them. Processing data streams is intricate due to several reasons: (i) the objects in the streams arrive online, (ii) the system has no control over the order in which objects arrive to be processed, either within a data stream or across data streams, (iii) data streams are potentially unbounded in size, and (iv) once an object from a data stream has been processed it is discarded or archived, it cannot be retrieved easily unless it is explicitly stored in memory, which typically is small relative to the size of the data streams [1].

For the past last decade, skyline query processing over data streams has attracted significant research attention in many emerging important applications. Although skyline computation for data streams has been studied extensively [5][7][12][15][16][17][22][23], there has been relatively less work on uncertain data stream. Uncertain data are defined as data which are inaccurate, imprecise, untrusted, and unknown. In fact, there is no work that focuses on uncertainty due to objects having interval values. The fast flowing of continuously generated data with uncertainty by an array of sources and devices complicates the query process and the amount of computations for processing the uncertain data stream is generally huge. It becomes more complicated when the values of the objects are nondeterministic, i.e., objects having interval values wherein the exact values of the objects are not known at the point of processing. For example, the prices of objects *a*, *b*, *d*, *e*, and *g* shown in Table 1 are in interval form. Here, one cannot derive the exact skyline but can only compute the probability of an object being a skyline member. In addition, identifying the domination between objects is not straightforward especially when the interval values of the objects intersect. For instance, one cannot state that object *a* dominates object *b* or object *b* dominates object *a* as the values of their prices intersect. Thus, identifying an efficient approach that is capable of computing skylines before the objects become obsolete to meet the time-critical expectancy of the applications is vital. It is also important to ensure that the approach can avoid the re-computation of probabilities of objects being skylines.

TABLE I: A SNAPSHOT OF SAMPLES OF DATA STREAM

Object	Price	Rating	Distance	…	Arrival Time (ms)
a	200 – 600	5	1.5		1
b	300 – 450	3	2.5		2
c	500	4	4.0		4
d	100 – 200	2	5.5		6
e	700 – 800	5	2.0		7
f	900	5	1.0		12
g	400 - 500	3	3.5		13

Hence, this paper attempts to tackle the issues of efficiently computing skyline over interval uncertain data stream. An approach that can handle uncertain data stream is proposed with the aim to reduce the cost of skyline computation while ensuring that the time-critical expectancy of applications is met. Two main tasks are identified, namely: clustering and skyline processing. Clustering technique is utilised to group objects that are similar into the same cluster. This will assist in identifying objects (clusters) that are dominated by other objects (clusters). The skyline processing is then employed to select the most dominant objects from each cluster and between clusters.

This paper is organised as follows: Section II presents the works related to the study. In Section III, definitions and notations that are used in the rest of the paper are set out. Our proposed approach is elaborated in Section IV. We have performed two analyses to evaluate the performance of our proposed approach. This is presented in Section V. Conclusion and future works are presented in the final section of this paper, Section VI.

II. RELATED WORK

Skyline query processing has been studied extensively for the last past decade. The earliest works focus on finding algorithm to expedite the process of identifying skylines for static dataset. These algorithms, which are based on non-indexing method include *Divide & Conquer (D&C)* [2], *Block Nested Loop (BNL)* [2], *Sort-Filter-Skyline (SFS)* [3], and *LESS* [6]. Then, algorithms using precompute indexes were proposed. These include *NN* [9], *Branch-and-Bound Skyline (BBS)* [17], and *ZSearch* [10]. There are also works that focus on uncertain data, such as *p-skyline*, which is designed for probabilistic skyline queries over static uncertain databases [18], *Iskyline* which supports skyline query on data that are represented as continuous ranges [8], and *SkyQUAD* a probabilistic skyline processing on interval values with threshold approach [19][20].

In the last decade, skyline query processing over data streams has attracted significant research attention in many emerging important applications, such as internet search logs, network traffic, sensor networks, and scientific data streams (such as in astronomic, genomics, physical simulations, etc.). In such applications, the challenge mainly lies in the huge volume of data, as well as its fast arrival rate. Moreover, it is impossible to reserve all the streaming items in memory, thus one-pass algorithms should be devised to adapt to the streaming data. Applying the existing methods of processing queries on this huge fast flowing data streams can be costly, time consuming, and impractical [1]. Several algorithms have been proposed for continuously monitoring skyline changes over ing data, which include *Lazy* and *Eager* algorithms [17], *LookOut* algorithm [16], and *FAST* algorithm [11]. On the other hand, the work by [12] focuses on skyline query of *n-of-N* data streams model in sliding window.

Recently, works have focused on processing skyline queries over uncertain data streams. This includes the work by [21] where skylines are identified based on objects having many varying instances with time. Works such as [24] and [4] have proposed efficient techniques in finding probabilistic skyline objects based on sliding windows on possible semantic. The work by [13] proposed the Effective Probability Skyline Update (*EPSU*) method by defining the interesting probabilistic skyline objects to return to the users and efficiently finding these objects without enumerating all possible objects. A sliding window partitioning strategy is proposed in [14] in order to reduce the processing time of the probability skyline computation. However, most of these works focus on objects having many instances. On the other hand, there is no work that identifies skyline over uncertain data stream, where uncertainty is due to objects having interval values.

III. PRELIMINARIES

In this section, we provide the definitions and notations that are related to skyline queries over uncertain data stream, which are necessary to clarify our proposed approach. Our approach has been developed in the context of multidimensional data stream, D, which consists of a set of objects, $D = \{o_1, o_2, o_3, \ldots\}$. An object of the database D is denoted by $o_i(d_1, d_2, \ldots, d_m)$ where o_i is the ith object with m-arity and $d = \{d_1, d_2, \ldots, d_m\}$ is the set of dimensions. In the following, we first give the general definitions that are related to skyline queries (Definitions 1 to Definition 5). Then, we extend these definitions to suit with uncertain data stream (Definitions 6 to Definition 9).

Definition 1 (Skyline): The set of skylines, S, is defined as those objects that are not dominated by any other objects in the dataset.

Definition 2 (Dominate): Given two objects o_i and $o_j \in D$ dataset with d dimensions, o_i dominates o_j (the lesser the better) (denoted by $o_i \prec o_j$) if and only if the following condition holds: $\forall\, d_k \in d,\ o_i.d_k \leq o_j.d_k \wedge \exists d_l \in d,\ o_i.d_l < o_j.d_l$.

Definition 3 (Skyline Queries): Select an object o_i from the set of objects D if and only if o_i is as good as o_j (where $i \neq j$) in all dimensions and *strictly* in at least one dimension. We use S to denote the set of skyline objects, $S = \{o_i \mid \forall\, o_i, o_j \in D, o_i \prec o_j\}$.

There are various forms of uncertain data. In this work, we focus on uncertain data where the object is expressed in an imprecise way, i.e., the exact value of the object is not known at the point of processing. This form of data is continuously generated especially in data stream.

Definition 4 (Uncertain Data): An object $o_i(d_1, d_2, \ldots, d_m)$ is said to contain uncertain data if at least one of its dimensions, d_j, contains value in the form of interval, i.e., $o_i[d_j] = [l, u]$ where l is the lower bound value and u is the upper bound value.

Definition 5 (Skyline over Uncertain Data) [19]: An object $o_i \in D$ with uncertain data is a skyline object if it has a probability of not being dominated by other object $o_j \in D$ more than a threshold value, H.

Figure 1(a) shows objects with exact values for dimensions price and distance. If we assumed minimum values are preferred in both dimensions, then the set of skyline objects returned is $\{m, l, k, j\}$. Meanwhile, Figure 1(b) shows examples of objects with interval values. In this example, we cannot state that object A definitely dominates object B, and vice versa, or that object F dominates object K with 100% probability.

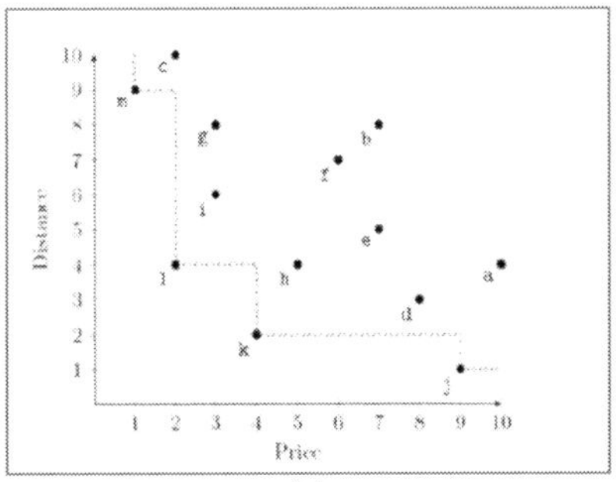

(a)

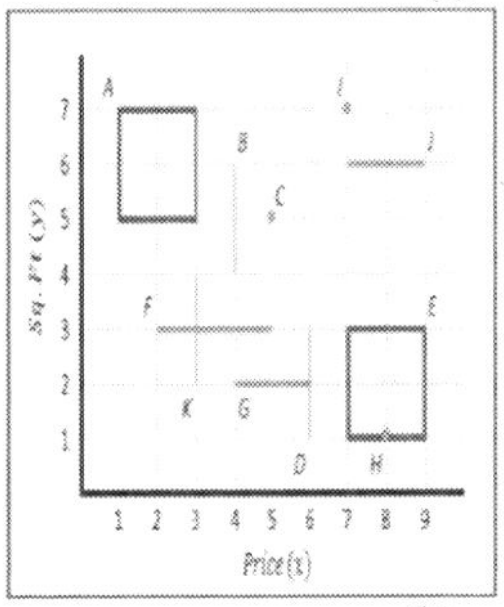

AptID	Price	Sq. Ft
A	1 - 3	5 - 7
B	4	4 - 6
C	5	5
D	6	1 - 3
E	7 - 9	1 - 3
F	2 - 5	3
G	4 - 6	2
H	8	1
I	7	7
J	7 - 9	6
K	3	2 - 4

(b)

Figure 1. (a) Skyline Example (b) Example of Uncertain Data [19]

Since a data stream is often unbounded, a query over a data stream is generally specified with a sliding window. The sliding-window model works based on recent objects of the data stream, whereas older objects are not taken into account, as they are considered obsolete.

Definition 6 (Data Stream): A data stream D contains a set of objects, $D = \{o_1, o_2, o_3, \ldots\}$ that arrive in sequence where each object is associated with a timestamp that indicates the arrival time of the object. We use the notation t_{oi} to indicate the arrival time of object o_i.

Definition 7 (Sliding Window) [11]: A sliding window, w_i, represents equally sized time intervals that are defined based on the parameters RANGE and SLIDE where RANGE specifies the length of the window extent and SLIDE specifies the step by which the window extent moves. Based on these parameters, the size of the sliding window can be easily determined.

Consider the hotel reservation systems where hotels continuously advertise their competitive deals to the system. The system contains streaming of millions of hotels for booking. Each hotel is associated with rating, distance from the city center, price etc. (see Table 1). The price advertised by the hotels might be in the form of exact value or within some price range. A potential user may ask the most preferable deals advertised during the recent 5 hours ($w3$ in Figure 2) and wants to update the results every 1 hour. In this example, RANGE = 5 and SLIDE = 1.

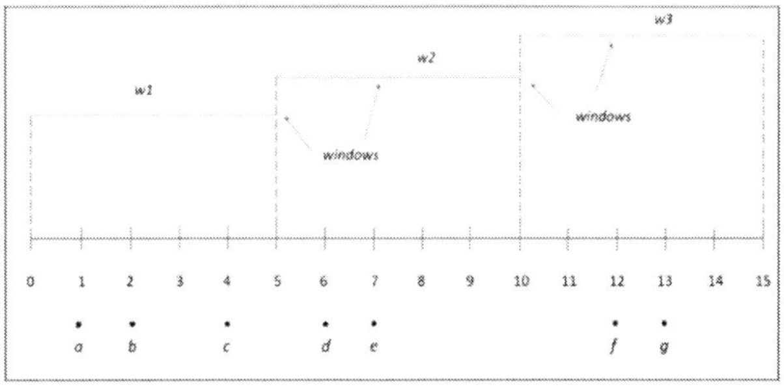

Figure 2. Sliding Windows [11]

Definition 8 (Skyline of a Sliding Window): The set of skylines of a window w_i, S_{wi}, is defined as those objects that are not dominated by any other objects in the window w_i.

Definition 9 (Skyline over Uncertain Data of a Sliding Window): An object of a given window, $o_i \in w_i$, with uncertain data is a skyline object if it has a probability of not being dominated by other object $o_j \in w_i$ more than a threshold value, H.

IV. THE PROPOSED APPROACH

Figure 3 presents our proposed approach in processing skyline queries over interval uncertain data stream. The proposed approach consists of four main stages, as explained below:

A. *Identifying the Sliding Windows of a Given Skyline Query*

Given a skyline query, SQ_q, the sliding window of the query is identified utilising the values of RANGE and SLIDE parameters. For each window, w_i, the objects that fall within the window are analysed. This is depicted in Figure 3(a). In this example, the second substream (window) contains 20 objects that are $A, B, C, \ldots, T$. Objects like B, E, J, M, N, O, P, R, S, and T contain interval values in the first dimension and are considered as uncertain.

B. *Grouping the Objects of a Sliding Window*

In this stage, objects are grouped based on the type of data they contain. Objects with exact values are grouped

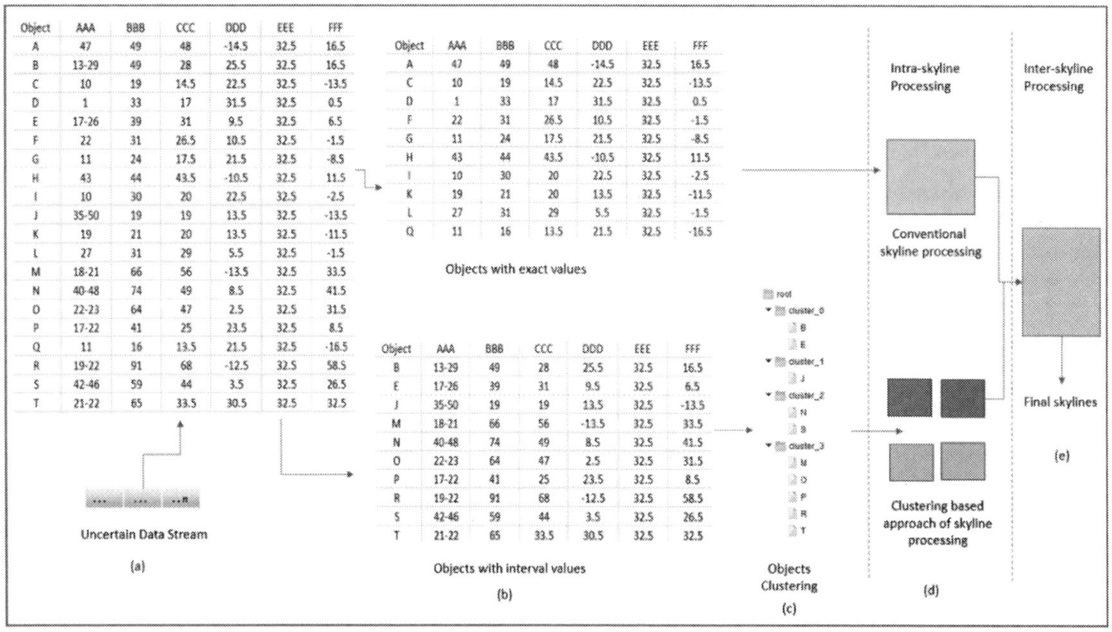

Figure 3. The Proposed Approach of Skyline Query Processing over Interval Uncertain Data Stream

together (G_A) while objects with interval values are put together in another group (G_R). This is shown in Figure 3(b). Based on the example, $G_A = \{A, C, D, F, G, H, I, K, L, Q\}$ and $G_R = \{B, E, J, M, N, O, P, R, S, T\}$.

C. *Clustering the Objects*

Objects in the G_R group are then clustered. In this work, the K-Means clustering technique is utilised. The objects are clustered only based on the dimension having interval values. Since the clustering technique requires deterministic values as input, thus the interval value of an object, for instance, $o_i[d_j] = [l, u]$, is represented by its mean value. We have performed several analyses, in which the interval value of an object is represented with its min, max, as well as mean value. Based on the analyses, representing the interval value with its mean value produces better set of clusters. However, due to limited space, the results of these analyses are not presented here. The result of this stage is a set of k-clusters denoted as $C = \{C_1, C_2, C_3, \ldots, C_k\}$. Figure 3(c) presents samples of clusters formed through this stage. There are four clusters for this example, labelled as *cluster_0*, *cluster_1*, *cluster_2*, and *cluster_3*.

D. *Identifying the Skylines*

In this final stage, the skylines are determined. Two levels of skyline processing are performed, namely: intra-skyline processing and inter-skyline processing.

Intra-skyline Processing – At this level, the candidate skylines are identified by comparing the objects within the group/cluster. The conventional skyline processing is utilised for the group of objects with exact values, i.e., those in the G_A group as shown in Figure 3(d). Here, the dominance comparison is performed at the object level. Based on the G_A derived from the second stage, object C dominates object I while object Q dominates object G. Both objects I and G are removed from further processing, while the other objects are considered as the candidate skylines of group G_A.

While those objects in the G_R group, the dominance comparison is performed at the cluster level instead of objects. Since the mean value is used to represent the interval value, thus the minimum (C_i-min) and maximum (C_i-max) mean values of a cluster are used to identify cluster domination, which is defined below:

Definition 10 (Cluster Domination): Given two clusters C_i and $C_j \in C$, C_i dominates C_j (denoted by $C_i \prec C_j$) if and only if the following condition hold: the C_i-max of $C_i < C_j$-min of C_j. C_i is called non-dominated cluster, while C_j is called dominated cluster.

Obviously, if a cluster, C_i, dominates a cluster C_j, this implies that the objects of cluster C_i dominate every object in cluster C_j. The objects of C_i are the candidate skylines. For example, comparing *cluster_0* = $\{B, E\}$ and *cluster_2* = $\{N, S\}$, the *cluster_0-max* = 21.5, which is less than the *cluster_2-min* = 44. This means that both objects B and E dominate objects N and S. A great number of probability computations can be avoided especially if the clusters contain a huge number of objects. However, since the cluster domination is only based on the dimension with interval values, the dominated clusters still have chances to be candidate skylines based on the other dimensions.

Nevertheless, it will not involve any probability computations.

Inter-skyline Processing – Here, the final skylines are identified by performing dominance comparison between the candidate skylines produced by conventional skyline processing and also those produced through the clustering domination. This means domination comparison is performed between the candidate skylines of G_A, non-dominated clusters, and dominated clusters. This is as shown by Figure 3(e).

V. EVALUATION

We have performed two simple analyses to get initial findings on the performance of our proposed approach. These analyses are conducted using RapidMiner [25] as a tool to cluster the objects. The first analysis aims to prove that at least one non-dominated cluster is identified. Having the non-dominated cluster implies that objects in the cluster can be omitted from further processing. The second analysis aims to prove that our proposed approach utilising the clustering technique can improve skyline processing by reducing the number of pairwise comparisons. For both analyses, we have varied the number of objects from 50 to 1000 objects. Every object has only a single dimension with interval values, which are generated randomly. Every interval value is within 20% of the range of possible values.

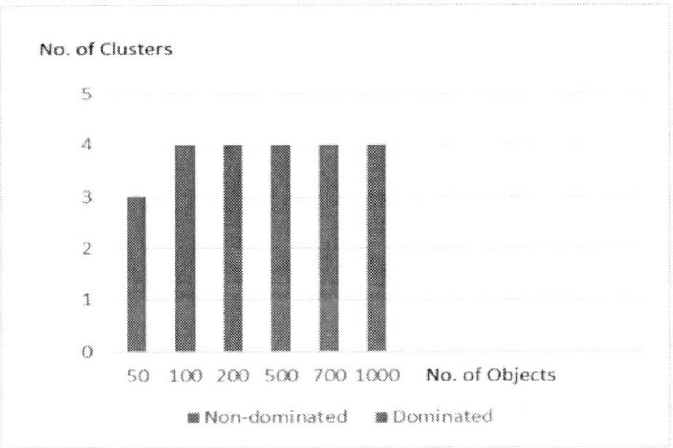

Figure 4. The Number of Non-dominated and Dominated Clusters

Figure 4 presents the results of the first analysis, which shows the number of non-dominated and dominated clusters formed when the number of objects varies from 50 to 1000. From this figure, the following can be observed:

(i) At least one non-dominated cluster is identified, which implies that the objects of the non-dominated cluster dominate the objects of the other clusters (dominated cluster).

(ii) The number of non-dominated clusters formed is not being affected by the number of objects. This can be clearly seen when the number of objects increased from 50 to 1000, the number of non-dominated cluster is always 1 (except for 200 objects).

(iii) Although the number of non-dominated and dominated clusters formed is almost the same when the number of objects varies from 50 to 1000, the number of objects in the clusters is not the same, i.e., the size of each cluster when the number of objects is 1000 is larger as compared to when the number of objects is 50.

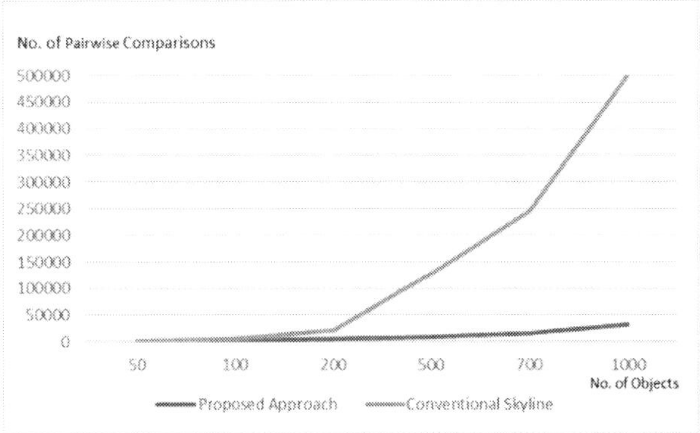

Figure 5. Number of Pairwise Comparisons

Figure 5 presents the results of the second analysis, which shows the number of pairwise comparisons performed by our proposed approach as compared to the conventional skyline processing approach. From the figure, the followings are observed:

(i) When the number of objects increases, the number of comparisons performed by our proposed approach increases steadily. While the number of comparisons performed by the conventional skyline approach shows a sudden increment as the number of objects increases.

(ii) On average the percentage of reduction with respect to number of pairwise comparisons gained by our proposed approach as compared to conventional skyline approach is 89.11%.

VI. CONCLUSION

This paper addresses the issues of processing skyline queries over interval uncertain data stream. An approach utilising the K-Means clustering technique has been proposed with the aim to reduce the number of pairwise comparisons. Two analyses have been conducted to get initial findings on the performance of the proposed approach. Results show that the approach is able to significantly reduce the number of pairwise comparisons. We will attempt to perform detailed analyses in the future to examine the proposed approach with regards to other aspects, such as scalability, distribution of interval values, and huge data size.

REFERENCES

[1] B. Babcock, S. Babu, M. Datar, R. Motwani, and J. Widom, "Models and issues in data stream systems,"

Proceedings of the Twenty-first ACM SIGMOD-SIGACT-SIGART Symposium on Principles of Database Systems, pp. 1 – 16, 2002.

[2] S. Borzsonyi, D. Kossmann, and K. Stocker, "The skyline operator," Proceedings of the 17th. International Conference on Data Engineering, pp. 421 – 430, 2001.

[3] J. Chomicki, P. Godfrey, J. Gryz, and D. Liang, "Skyline with presorting: theory and optimizations," Proceedings of the Intelligent Information Processing and Web Mining, pp. 595 – 604, 2005.

[4] X. Ding, X. Lian, L. Chen, and H. Jin, "Continuous monitoring of skylines over uncertain data streams," Journal of Information Sciences, vol. 184(1), Feb. 2012, pp. 196 – 214, doi:10.1016/j.ins.2011.09.007.

[5] L. Dong, G. Liu, X. Cui, and T. Li, "Finding group-based skyline over a data stream in the sensor network," Journal of Information, vol. 9(2), Feb. 2018, pp. 1 – 22, doi:10.3390/info9020033.

[6] P. Godfrey, R. Shipley, and J. Gryz, "Maximal vector computation in large data sets," Proceedings of the 31st. International Conference on Very large Data Bases, pp. 229 – 240, 2005.

[7] X. Guo, H. Li, A. Wulamu, Y. Xie, and Y. Fu, "Efficient processing of skyline group queries over a data stream," Journal of Tsinghua Science Technology, vol. 21(1), Feb. 2016, pp. 29 – 39, doi: 0.1109/TST.2016.7399281.

[8] M. E. Khalefa, M. F. Mokbel, and J. J. Levandoski, "Skyline query processing for uncertain data," Proceedings of the 19th. ACM International Conference on Information and Knowledge Management, pp. 1293 – 1296, 2010.

[9] D. Kossmann, F. Ramsak, and S. Rost, "Shooting stars in the sky: An online algorithm for skyline queries," Proceedings of the 28th. International Conference on Very Large Data Bases, pp. 275 – 286, 2002.

[10] K. C. Lee, W. C. Lee, B. Zheng, H. Li, and Y. Tian, "Z-SKY: An efficient skyline query processing framework based on z-order," Journal of Very Large Data Bases, vol. 19(3), June 2010, pp. 333 – 362, doi:10.1007/s00778-009-0166-x.

[11] Y. W. Lee, K. Y. Lee, and M. H. Kim, "Efficient processing of multiple continuous skyline queries over a data stream," Journal of Information Sciences, vol. 221, Feb. 2013, pp. 316 – 337, doi: 10.1016/j.ins.2012.09.040.

[12] X. Lin, Y. Yuan, W. Wang, and H. Lu, "Stabbing the sky: efficient skyline computation over sliding windows," Proceedings of the 21st. International Conference on Data Engineering (ICDE '05), pp. 502 – 513, 2005.

[13] C. Liu and S. Tang, "An effective probabilistic skyline query process on uncertain data streams," Proceedings of the 6th. International Conference on Emerging Ubiquitous Systems and Pervasive Networks, pp. 40 – 47, 2015.

[14] J. Liu, X. Li, K. Ren, J. Song, and Z. Zhang, "Parallel n-of-N skyline queries over uncertain data streams," Proceedings of the International Conference on Database and Expert Systems Applications, pp. 176 – 184, 2018.

[15] H. Lu, Y. Zhou, and J. Haustad, "Efficient and scalable continuous skyline monitoring in two-tier streaming settings," Journal of Information Systems, vol. 38(1), Mac 2013, 68 –81, doi: 10.1016/j.is.2012.05.005.

[16] M. Morse, J. M. Patel, and W. I. Grosky, "Efficient continuous skyline computation," Journal of Information Sciences, vol. 177(17), Sept. 2007, pp. 3411 – 3437, doi: 10.1016/j.ins.2007.02.033.

[17] D. Papadias, Y. Tao, G. Fu, and B. Seeger, "Progressive skyline computation in database systems," Journal of ACM Transactions on Database Systems (TODS), vol. 30(1), Mar. 2005, pp. 41 – 82, doi: 10.1145/1061318.1061320.

[18] J. Pei, B. Jiang, X. Lin, and Y. Yuan, "Probabilistic skylines on uncertain data," Proceedings of the 33rd. International Conference on Very Large Data Bases, pp. 15 –26, 2007.

[19] N. H. M. Saad, H. Ibrahim, A. A. Alwan, F. Sidi, and R. Yakoob, "A framework for evaluating skyline query over uncertain autonomous databases," Proceedings of the International Conference of Computational Science (ICCS 2014), pp. 1546-1556, 2014.

[20] N. H. M. Saad, H. Ibrahim, A. A. Alwan, F. Sidi, and R. Yakoob, "Computing range skyline query on uncertain dimension," Proceedings of the Database and Expert System Applications (DEXA), pp. 377 – 388, 2016.

[21] H. Z. Su, E. T. Wang, and A. L. Chen, "Continuous probabilistic skyline queries over uncertain data streams," Proceedings of the International Conference on Database and Expert Systems Applications, pp. 105 – 121, 2010.

[22] Z. Wang, J. Xin, L. Ding, J. Ba, and X. Gao, "ρ-Dominant skyline computation on data stream," Journal of IEEE Access, vol. 6, Sept. 2018, pp. 53201 – 53213, doi:10.1109/ACCESS.2018.2871254.

[23] J. Xin, G. Wang, L. Chen, X. Zhang, and Z. Wang, "Continuously maintaining sliding window skylines in a sensor network," Proceedings of the International Conference on Database Systems for Advanced Applications, pp. 509 – 521, 2007.

[24] W. Zhang, A. Li, M. A. Cheema, Y. Zhang, and L. Chang, "Probabilistic n-of-N skyline computation over uncertain data streams," Journal of World Wide Web, vol. 18(5), Sept. 2015, pp. 1331 – 1350, doi:10.1007/s11280-014-0292-2.

[25] https://rapidminer.com/. Last accessed 21 February 2019.

Towards a Knowledge Graph to Describe and Process Data Defects

João Marcelo Borovina Josko*, Lisa Ehrlinger†‡, Wolfram Wöß†
*Federal University of ABC, Av. dos Estados, 5001 Bairro Santa Terezinha – Santo André, Brazil
email: marcelo.josko@ufabc.edu.br
†Johannes Kepler University Linz, Altenberger Straße 69, 4040 Linz, Austria
email: lisa.ehrlinger@jku.at, wolfram.woess@jku.at
‡Software Competence Center Hagenberg, Softwarepark 21, 4232 Hagenberg, Austria
email: lisa.ehrlinger@scch.at

Abstract—**The reliability and trustworthiness of machine learning models depends directly on the data used to train them. Knowledge about data defects that affect machine learning models is most often considered implicitly by data analysts, but usually no centralized data defect management exists. Knowledge graphs are a powerful tool to capture, structure, evolve, and share semantics about data defects. In this paper, we present an ontology to describe data defects and demonstrate its applicability to build a large public or enterprise knowledge graph.**

Keyword Terms— Data Defects; Data Quality Assessment; Knowledge Graphs.

I. Introduction

If the data used for Machine Learning (ML) applications has defects, the resulting ML model will perform poorly and generate unreliable results. Possible effects are cost increase, incorrect decision making, customer dissatisfaction, and organizational mistrust within organizations [1]. Examples for data defects, which have received increased attention in the ML community, are missing data (by error) and outlying values [2]. However, knowledge about such defects is almost always tacit within organizations and concentrated on a few data professionals that may have an incomplete understanding of all data defect implications and characteristics. Knowledge Graphs (KGs) bear the potential to capture, structure, evolve, and share semantics about data defects, which constitutes the basis for comprehensive Data Quality (DQ) management for ML applications. DQ is most often associated with the "fitness for use" principle [3][4], which highlights the importance of taking into account the respective context and the consumer (i.e., user or service) of the data. While there has been a lot discussion on Data Quality Assessment (DQA) in general (cf. [1][5][6]), and data defects in particular (cf. [7]–[9]), an analysis of the literature reveals a segmented representation of data defect knowledge.

KGs, which are defined to "acquire and integrate information into an ontology and apply a reasoner to derive new knowledge" [10], have already been successfully applied to organize the semantic information of different domains, like scientific documents [11][12]. However, so far, there exists no KG to describe data defects. To address this gap, we present a KG model in form of an ontology to represent the semantic information of data defects and show how to apply it to public or enterprise KGs, i.e., how to populate such a KG. The main contribution of this paper is an ontology that allows a practitioner to know *which* knowledge about data defects is required and *how* to organize it. The high expressiveness of ontologies [13] allows to incorporate the context (cf. fitness-for-use principle of DQ [3]) of the data defects within the model, such as the function or database (DB) table where a defect occurs.

This paper is structured in three parts: Section II provides an overview on related work. Section III comprises a theoretical introduction to data defects, the discussion of our ontology, and its applicability. We conclude in Section IV.

II. Related Work

DQ literature provides huge knowledge about data defects, with certain papers discussing topics like data defect structures [7][8][14], methods of data defect detection [6], DQ dimensions [1][6][3] and DQA process characterization [1][5][9]. Despite their considerable contribution, no attention has been paid to represent the relationships among data defect concepts and the situation they appear in (i.e., context). In ML applications, explicit knowledge about data defects, like missing or outlying values, would enhance prediction accuracy. To incorporate knowledge about data defects into ML models, it is thus necessary, to describe it semantically.

KGs have already been successfully applied to describe complex domains like science [11][12] or the Italien cultural heritage within the ArCo project [15]. Following this line, some works provide a semantic description of the DQ assessment domain, observing the topic from a general [16] or domain-specific [17] perspective (e.g., linked data). However, these works focus on the task of assessing or measuring DQ and do not go into detail to describe specific data defects. In this paper, we provide a machine-readable semantic representation of the data defect domain, which provides on the one hand a standardized and centralized repository about data defects and their handling, and on the other hand, allows to incorporate this knowledge into automated ML workflows.

III. A Knowledge Graph to Describe Data Defects

In this section, we (1) explain the theory behind data defects, (2) present an ontology on data defects, which constitutes the structure of a KG, and (3) demonstrate how to apply this ontology and build a public or enterprise KG.

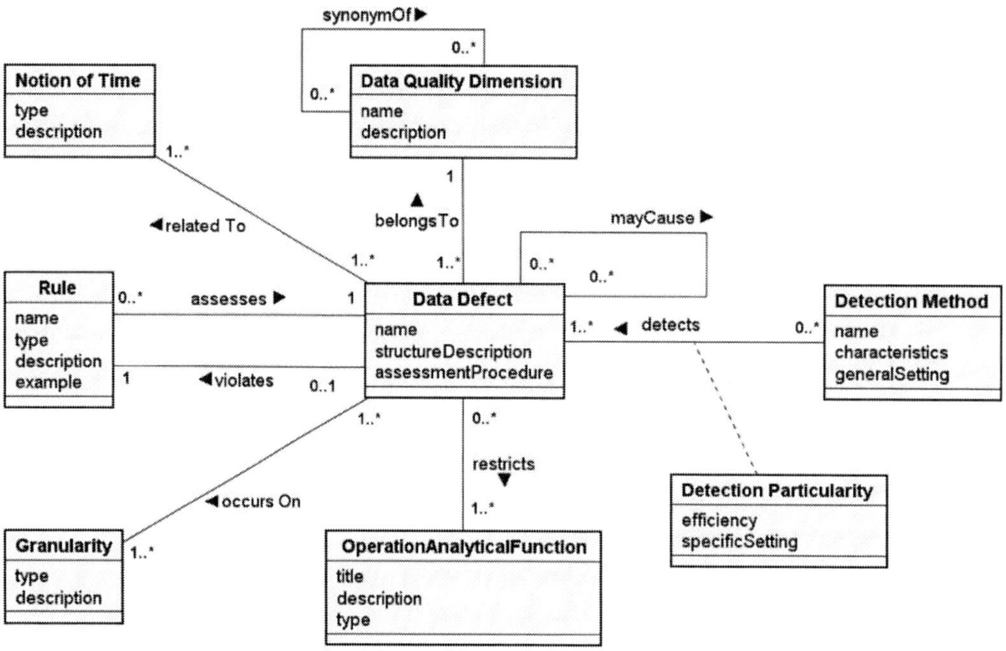

Fig. 1. An ontology to represent the data defect domain

A. Theory on Data Defects

In a nutshell, a data defect is a disagreement between what is provided by a database and what is expected from it according to some data semantic. Such disagreement results from rule violations like organizational business rules (e.g., domain rule, tax rules) or database implicit rules (e.g., databases should not have duplicates) [9]. The way in which a rule is violated denotes the structure of a particular data defect [8].

Data defects also share some implicit properties. The first property refers to *inherently complex nature*. A data defect occurs in more than one granularity (e.g., value, tuple, column, relation), and its core structure may possess slight variations or particularities. Moreover, in certain data settings, a data defect $\mathcal{D}_A$ may cause a defect $\mathcal{D}_B$ and, progressively, lead to a chain reaction [5]. This situation can be especially critical in the case of temporal data.

The next property refers to *level of human supervision* required to determine a data defect [5]. While some defects can be automatically determined through assessment rules (as used by data profiling tools), other data defects require knowledge about a particular business context to be refuted or confirmed. In any case, each data defect demands a particular assessment analysis procedure.

As the last property, data defects can also cause distinct *impacts on data life cycle operations* (e.g., use, maintain or purge data) and, consequently, operational and analytical functions they are part of. Certain defects may totally obstruct one or more functionalities such as credit concession blockage for certain customer on account of an incorrect income value. In contrast, other "less severe" data defects do not inhibit functionalities, but they "use" them to proliferate defective data all around organizational databases. An example of this case refers to determine product discounts based on incorrect customers ranking.

B. The Data Defect Ontology

Figure 1 shows the ontology (diagrammed in UML) that provides concepts and constructs for specifying, organizing, evolving, and communicating semantic content about data defects, according to data defects properties (Section III-A). Its key concept is *Data Defect*. It represents a violation of a *Rule* that leads to defective data. Conversely, a rule (or set of rules) may be used to discover a data defect. Moreover, a data defect belongs to a particular *Data Quality Dimension* (e.g., accuracy, consistency, as proposed in [3]) and refers to some *Notion (Dimension) of Time* like snapshot, valid time and transactional time [7].

The connection to the data is provided by the concept of *Granularity*, which defines a specific granularity of the data, where a data defect can occur on (e.g., value, tuple, column, or relation in a database). This granularity can for example be specified with a SQL statement that links to the affected data.

The presence of defective data has the potential to restrict the use of a number of *Operational and Analytical Functions* (OperationalAnalyticalFunction). Besides these impacts, the ontology also models impacts between data defects, i.e., the fact that certain data defects may trigger other data defects. The current version does not contain the impact of the user or service using the data, which is part of our future work.

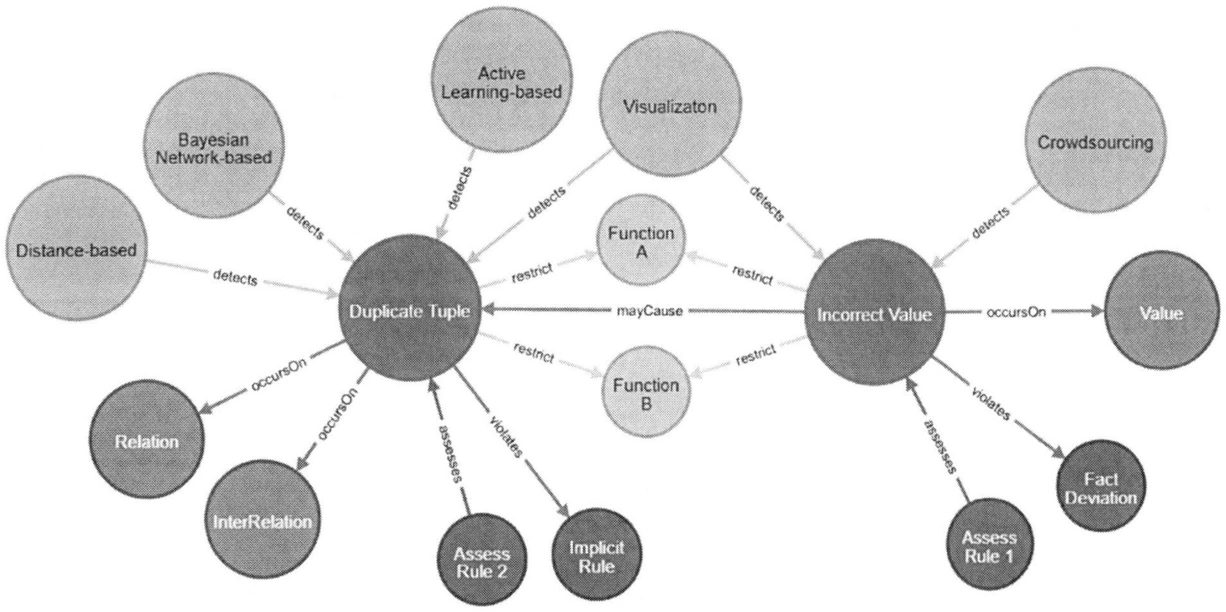

Fig. 2. A KG prototype for the data defect domain

A *Detection Method* can reveal a specific set of data defects, but with different efficiency and configuration setting (*Detection Particularity*). However, each data defect has a particular human assessment analysis procedure (*assessmentProcedure*). Further, a data defect can occur on one ore more granularity levels, such as values, tuples, columns, or relations. On the one hand, defects can be assessed through rules (*Rule*), which are, e.g., used by data profiling tools. On the other hand, data defects can be characterized by the rules they violate. This interrelation is modeled by the two relationships between rules and data defects.

Our model does not intend to represent semantically expected data volatility situations (e.g., missing data values that do not exist in the real world) since they do not represent a data defect (cf. Section III-A). In addition we want to point out that the focus of our research is on DQ assessment (detection, measurement) and automatic data cleansing activities are not in the scope of this research work. However, it is necessary to measure and know the quality of the data to understand the degree and effectiveness of data cleansing and to define goals for further cleansing activities [18][19]. The incorporation of data cleansing is planned in future work, but it requires a deeper investigation of data cleansing methods to expand the model appropriately.

C. Application with a Knowledge Graph Prototype

To demonstrate the applicability of our data defect ontology, we built a KG prototype using the Neo4J graph database [20]. Figure 2 shows an exemplary query result that highlights the consistency and clarity provided by the data defect ontology. In order to keep Figure 2 readable, the query has been restricted to a subset of properties and concepts about two notorious data defects: *Duplicate Tuples* and *Incorrect Values*. Further details about these and other timeless data defects are discussed in [8].

Each node color in Figure 2 corresponds to one concept expressed in the data defect ontology (cf. Section III-B) and each edge color corresponds to its source node color and the label exhibits its role. We used the following color code:

- Red: data defect
- Blue: rule
- Purple: granularity
- Brown: operational-analytical function
- Green: detection method

The nomenclature used for the labels of the nodes for data defects (red), granularity (purple), and detection method (green), exhibit name-based attributes that are notorious in database literature like [2][8]. Further information on the two data defects *Duplicate Tuples* and *Incorrect Values* is provided in [8]. A *Relation* refers to a table in a relational database, *InterRelation* to a join between two or more tables, and a *Value* to one specific value within a table (e.g., a integer, string, or boolean). While general information on different data defect detection methods is reviewed by Dasu and Johnson [9], methods specifically attributed to duplicate detection are summarized by Elmagarmid et al. [21]. A few examples are *Distance-based* methods, which are based on a function that calculates the distance between two objects [21], *Bayesian-Network-based* methods, which compute the conditional dependencies between objects (variables) using probabilistic inference [22], *Active-Learning-based* methods that rely on ML methods, *Visualization* as important tool for detection data defects (as highlighted in [23]), and *Crowdsourcing*.

Since business rules and operational-analytical functions (cf. Section III-A) rely on the domain context, their corresponding nodes in Figure 2 (blue and brown respectively) use fictional labels, e.g., "Assess Rule 1", or "Function A". To maintain the figure readable and demonstrative, we did not include *Notion of Time* in the current version.

IV. Conclusion and Future Work

This paper introduces an ontology to represent semantic knowledge about data defects, which extends the W3C DQ vocabulary [16]. The design of the ontology considers several data defect properties and its applicability was examined by means of a KG prototype. Such a knowledge graph enables organizations to acquire, organize, evolve, and promote a common understanding of data defects within their domain. In future works, we intend to (1) investigate how knowledge regarding the data defects domain can be captured automatically, (2) additionally take into account the impact on DQ from the user or service utilizing the data, and (3) extend our ontology to fully support spatial data defects. The latter refers to the ability to full express data defects semantics with respect to relationships among distinct spatial attributes (e.g., location, shape, size, and orientation) that are not properly captured by *Granularity*, for instance.

Acknowledgment

The research reported in this paper has been partly supported by the Austrian Ministry for Transport, Innovation and Technology, the Federal Ministry of Digital and Economic Affairs, and the Province of Upper Austria in the frame of the COMET center SCCH.

References

[1] T. C. Redman, "The impact of poor data quality on the typical enterprise," *Communications of the ACM*, vol. 41, no. 2, 1998, pp. 79–82.

[2] C. C. Aggarwal, *Outlier analysis*. Springer International Publishing, 2017.

[3] R. Y. Wang and D. M. Strong, "Beyond accuracy: What data quality means to data consumers," *Journal of Management Information Systems*, vol. 12, no. 4, March 1996, pp. 5–33.

[4] N. R. Chrisman, "The role of quality information in the long-term functioning of a geographic information system," *Cartographica: The International Journal for Geographic Information and Geovisualization*, vol. 21, no. 2, 1983, pp. 79–88.

[5] J. M. Borovina Josko, "Uso de propriedades visuais-interativas na avaliação da qualidade de dados (in portuguese)," Ph.D. thesis, Universidade de São Paulo, 2016.

[6] D. Loshin, *The practitioner's guide to data quality improvement*. Elsevier, 2010.

[7] J. M. Borovina Josko, "A formal taxonomy of temporal data defects," in *Data Quality and Trust in Big Data*, H. Hacid, Q. Z. Sheng, T. Yoshida, A. Sarkheyli, and R. Zhou, Eds. Cham: Springer International Publishing, 2019, pp. 94–110.

[8] J. M. Borovina Josko, M. K. Oikawa, and J. E. Ferreira, "A formal taxonomy to improve data defect description," in *International Conference on Database Systems for Advanced Applications*. Springer, 2016, pp. 307–320.

[9] T. Dasu, "Data glitches: Monsters in your data," in *Handbook of Data Quality*. Heidelberg, Germany: Springer, 2013, pp. 163–178.

[10] L. Ehrlinger and W. Wöß, "Towards a definition of knowledge graphs," in *Joint Proceedings of the Posters and Demos Track of 12th International Conference on Semantic Systems - SEMANTiCS2016 and 1st International Workshop on Semantic Change & Evolving Semantics (SuCCESS16)*, ser. CEUR Workshop Proceedings, E. F. Michael Martin, Martí Cuquet, Ed., vol. 1695, Aachen, 2016, pp. 13–16.

[11] S. Auer, V. Kovtun, M. Prinz, A. Kasprzik, M. Stocker, and M. E. Vidal, "Towards a knowledge graph for science," in *Proceedings of the 8th International Conference on Web Intelligence, Mining and Semantics (WIMS '18)*. New York, NY, USA: ACM, 2018, pp. 1:1–1:6.

[12] S. Fathalla, S. Vahdati, S. Auer, and C. Lange, "Towards a knowledge graph representing research findings by semantifying survey articles," in *International Conference on Theory and Practice of Digital Libraries*. Springer, 2017, pp. 315–327.

[13] C. Feilmayr and W. Wöß, "An analysis of ontologies and their success factors for application to business," *Data & Knowledge Engineering*, vol. 101, 2016, pp. 1–23.

[14] E. Rahm and H. H. Do, "Data cleaning: Problems and current approaches," *IEEE Data Engineering Bulletin*, vol. 23, no. 4, 2000, pp. 3–13.

[15] L'Istituto Centrale per il catalogo e la Documentazione (ICCD), "ArCo," 2019, https://github.com/ICCD-MiBACT/ArCo [retrieved: May, 2019].

[16] R. Albertoni and A. Isaac, "Data on the web best practices: Data quality vocabulary," *W3C Working Draft*, vol. 19, 2016.

[17] J. Debattista, C. Lange, and S. Auer, "daq, an ontology for dataset quality information," in *Linked Data on the Web (LDOW)*, 2014.

[18] L. Sebastian-Coleman, *Measuring Data Quality for Ongoing Improvement: A Data Quality Assessment Framework*. Newnes, 2012.

[19] L. Ehrlinger, B. Werth, and W. Wöß, "Automated Continuous Data Quality Measurement with QualIe," *International Journal on Advances in Software*, vol. 11, no. 3 & 4, 2018, pp. 400–417.

[20] J. J. Miller, "Graph database applications and concepts with Neo4j," in *Proceedings of the Southern Association for Information Systems Conference, Atlanta, GA, USA*, vol. 2324, 2013.

[21] A. K. Elmagarmid, P. G. Ipeirotis, and V. S. Verykios, "Duplicate record detection: A survey," *IEEE Transactions on Knowledge and Data Engineering*, vol. 19, no. 1, 2007, pp. 1–16.

[22] D. Koller and N. Friedman, *Probabilistic graphical models: principles and techniques*. MIT press, 2009.

[23] C. Bors, T. Gschwandtner, S. Kriglstein, S. Miksch, and M. Pohl, "Visual interactive creation, customization, and analysis of data quality metrics," *Journal of Data and Information Quality (JDIQ)*, vol. 10, no. 1, 2018, p. 3.